THE GOLDSBORO BROKEN ARROW

THE GOLDSBORO BROKEN ARROW

THE B-52 CRASH OF
JANUARY 24, 1961
GOLDSBORO, NORTH CAROLINA

THE STORY OF THE MEN ON THE SHARP END

BY
JOEL DOBSON

Copyright 2011 Joel Dobson

ISBN 978-1-257-76914-8

*I know not with which weapons World War III will be fought,
but World War IV will be fought with sticks and stones.*
Albert Einstein

Now, I am become Death, the destroyer of worlds.
As quoted from the *Bhagavad Gītā*
by J. Robert Oppenheimer at the Trinity Site.

Everybody grab a throttle and run forward.
Take off announcement made by unknown B-52 pilot.

DEDICATION

This book is dedicated to Adam Columbus Mattocks, a man ahead of his time. He was a professional United States Air Force officer, a skilled pilot; a black man in the South in the 1960s. He was a member of the Strategic Air Command in a difficult time when his country needed him. He was willing to go into harm's way, and was on *the point of the spear*. But most of all, he was a gentle, Christian man, whose only thoughts during his time of crisis were of his family and of his Maker.

CONTENTS

List of Illustrations xi
Foreword, by Dr. Roy Heidicker xiii
Author's Preface xv
Acknowledgments xix

Prologue xxvii

Part I. 1
Chapter 1. The Crew and Their Plane 3
Chapter 2. The Mission 25
Chapter 3. The Bail Out 55
Chapter 4. The Crash Site 65
Chapter 5. The Chance of Nuclear Detonation 89
Chapter 6. The Cause of the Crash 107

Part II. 119
Chapter 7. After Goldsboro 121

Afterword, by Lt. Col. Wilton Strickland, USAF (Ret) 143
Appendix A. The Crewmembers 145
Appendix B. "This Is What It Was Like," Major Tulloch's Narrative .. 147
Appendix C. Findings of Accident Board 155
Appendix D. Table of Component Behavior 157

Appendix E. Lists of Broken Arrows (DOD, as of 1980) Maggelet & Oskins 159

Appendix F. Bomb Locations, Faro 161

Notes **165**

Bibliography of References **185**

ILLUSTRATIONS

The BUFF

Major Walter Tulloch, Aircraft Commander

Captain Dick Rardin, Copilot

Lieutenant Bill Wilson, Electronic Warfare Officer

Sergeant Frank Barnish, Gunner

Major Gene Shelton, Radar Navigator

Captain Paul Brown, Navigator

Crew Positions

Major Richards' Seat

B-52 Landing

Chrome Dome Southern Routes

Lieutenant Adam Mattocks, Third Pilot

Major Eugene Richards

Bail Out Routes

Ejection Seat Trigger

"Night Scene Over Faro: The Crash of *Keep 19*"

Scott and Betty Tulloch, on Their Wedding Day

Debris Field, Faro, North Carolina

First Lieutenant Jack ReVelle

Bomb One, In the Trees on Shackleford Road

EOD Team from Wright-Patterson AFB

Retrieval of Parachute Pack, Bomb Two

Wing Removal

Crash Site, 1961

Crash Site, 2011

Impact of MK-39, on Manhattan

Schematic of MK-39 Type Weapon

The Three Graves

Adam Mattocks at 50th Anniversary, at Site

Jack ReVelle Returns to Bomb Site One

Bomb in Trees, 1961

Nahunta Swamp Bridge and Site Easement

EOD Team, Seymour Johnson, with Jack ReVelle

FOREWORD

Dr. Roy Heidicker, Wing Historian, 4th Fighter Wing

In 2005 I arrived in Goldsboro, North Carolina, at Seymour Johnson Air Force Base. I soon discovered that as an Air Force historian I had struck gold in the 4th Fighter Wing. Their heritage, from the Eagle Squadrons through today, is unsurpassed in the history of the United States Air Force.

I also discovered that even though I was the Wing and not the base historian, I would be asked a lot of questions about the history of Seymour Johnson. One particular question kept coming up again and again. Many people wanted me to tell them about the crash of the B-52 bomber in 1961 that involved two nuclear bombs. But the questions were often phrased in such a way that I soon realized the person asking knew a lot about the crash but they wanted me to answer the questions: "What really happened?" and "Why won't the Air Force tell people that a live nuclear bomb is buried in Faro, North Carolina?".

I found a Web site that dealt with the crash so I was able to answer questions in a more informed manner. But I also realized that my answers to *the bomb* questions never really satisfied the person asking the question. This was the case for several years. Although I didn't intend it, some people probably looked at me as being part of the great B-52 crash conspiracy. Then in 2011 something wonderful happened. It was the fiftieth anniversary of the crash and a reunion of people involved in the crash met in Faro, North Carolina. As the Wing historian I was invited to attend this event. Joel Dobson, who was finishing a book about the crash, put together the event. I spoke with Joel and enjoyed his presentation at the reunion. Joel, a former officer in the Strategic Air Command, has now written the go-to source for questions regarding the Goldsboro B-52 crash in 1961.

He has gone through the records, interviewed the participants, and grilled the experts. This fine book is the last word on this event. There are no stones left unturned because Joel Dobson has turned them all. In addition to answering all the questions, Joel's book is a great story well told about brave Americans dealing with an unbelievable crisis. The Goldsboro Broken Arrow could have been the greatest man-made disaster in the history of North America. Instead it is an edge-of-your-seat tale about close calls and disaster averted. Everyone in eastern North Carolina owes a debt of gratitude to Joel Dobson for finally revealing "what really happened," and answering "Why won't the Air Force tell people that a live nuclear bomb is buried in Faro, North Carolina?". But seriously, the most grateful person is me. From now on when people want to grill me about the crash I will direct them to this fine book.

AUTHOR'S PREFACE

I first got interested in this story when my son told me about the *lost bomb* of Goldsboro, a nuclear bomb supposedly buried somewhere near Goldsboro, North Carolina. I had been an Air Force lieutenant in the Strategic Air Command (SAC) back in the 1960s, but I had never heard of this 1961 B-52 accident. A Broken Arrow is an accident or incident involving a nuclear weapon with the potential for detonation. The closest I had been to a Broken Arrow was the time I almost triggered an alert when I was Officer Of The Day on the SAC base where I was stationed, but luckily it never reached the point of alert. I had received a call from the tower that "an aircraft was burning on the flight line." We only had B-58s, and all of them were probably loaded for bear. If one was burning it could have nukes aboard, and I would be the lucky one to kick off an unstoppable telephone alert for the base. As I was pondering the written procedures, a second call reported that it was only a transient Marine Corps jet fighter that had landed with a collapsed landing gear, and was still sliding down the runway emitting sparks. No harm, no foul. The Broken Arrow recall alert was not necessary.

I have lived in North Carolina for thirty years now, and I figured it would be interesting to check out this *Goldsboro bomb* on our way back from a family beach trip. Little did I realize what I was getting into.

That 1961 accident of a B-52 in Goldsboro, and the lessons learned from it, is the subject of this book. Two thermonuclear bombs fell from the plane, and I look at just how close we came to a major disaster, a nuclear detonation on United States soil, hundreds of times larger than that of Hiroshima. The book also briefly looks at some of the other incredible nuclear accidents such as Chernobyl and Fukushima, and the inherent dangers that lie within. I do not attempt to cover all the details of all Broken Arrow incidents, because that has already been done, and done well by such people as Mike Maggelet and Jim Oskins. I am by no means an expert in any of this, just someone who wants to pass on to my grandchildren what happened then, and what could have happened, because I believe that Nature has a simple rule: The Lesson will be repeated until it is learned.

Over the subsequent fifty years since the Goldsboro incident different people using the Freedom of Information Act (FOIA) have obtained various pieces of information, and thus some key government reports were released. Some of the reports have redacted words or lines, which means some portions are blacked out, but they still made for intriguing reading. I began to assemble the bits and pieces and to dig into the details of the crash. There has never been a book, as far as I can tell, about this accident. I did find a Web site started by four University of North Carolina students at Chapel Hill as part of a class requirement. That led me to the Web site team leader, Cliff Nelson, who had interviewed several interesting people, such as Ralph Lapp, Daniel Ellsberg, and Chuck Hansen.

Cliff made me aware of this phrase, which will surely grab your attention: ". . . largest man-made disaster in history . . ." This phrase had been the source of some controversy for several years, and while it is not my intent to settle that or any other controversy here, at least I can report on them. *The Stockholm Peace Research Institute Yearbook* of 1977 evidently based the statement on an erroneous calculation in 1961 by Dr. Lapp when he called the bomb twenty-four megatons. Then I found out that would have been bigger than anything in the US nuclear inventory at the time.

Later research reported the Goldsboro bomb as 2.4 megatons, a far cry from twenty-four. But that did not make it any less comforting to know that even a 2.4-megaton bomb would exceed the yield of all munitions (outside of testing) ever detonated in the history of the world by TNT, gunpowder, conventional bombs, and the Hiroshima and Nagasaki blasts combined.

The hunt was on. The bomb turned out to be 3.8 megatons, big enough to have a kill zone of seventeen miles according to the man who deactivated it. And part of one bomb still is buried at Faro, in a field twelve miles north of Goldsboro. I joined the B-52 Association and began to make contacts and get the stories of those who flew the B-52, and those who maintained it and its weapons. I asked for and received all available military records of crewmembers from the National Records Center in St. Louis, Missouri.

A thirty-day vacation around the western part of the country included places like the SAC Museum in Ashland, Nebraska; STRATCOM (Strategic Command), formerly SAC headquarters in Omaha; the B-52 museum sites in Denver, Colorado, and Big Springs, Texas; and Los Alamos and Santa Fe, New Mexico, where the Manhattan Project was formed. My wife and I also visited three specific gravesites along the way. And then I found the last surviving member of the crew, the third pilot, Adam Mattocks, and the man who deactivated both bombs, Jack ReVelle.

This book consists of what I found out about the men of that flight, *Keep 19*, how that mission developed through the strange thought process that was the Strategic Air Command, and what the consequences were. It also contains the stories of the people of Faro, North Carolina, and how they dealt with the fire that rained down on them that night of January 23, 1961. Interviews with individuals are noted in the text, as well as personal experiences. I cite those sources that I consider to be noteworthy, but do not attempt to make this a scholarly thesis, citing every source. My intent is to make this an interesting read about something important that happened in my lifetime.

The timing of this book is both fortunate and unfortunate. It is fortunate in that so many previously classified pieces of information are now declassified and available. It is unfortunate in that so many of the people involved in the event are now getting along in years. It is time to write their stories down.

The far-reaching story is about how we as a nation arrived at that point in time when we were ready and willing to sacrifice everything based on what we thought we knew to be right. The Strategic Air Command does not exist anymore, but the B-52 still flies. There remains a remnant of that time in the ground at Faro. We have learned a few things since 1961, but we are still running up against the consequences of decisions. We still have to deal with the results of Chernobyl and now its twin sister, Fukushima.

This is the story of how that one accident happened in 1961, how the bomb site was located, and how people involved in an event fifty years ago got together fifty years later at the place where it all happened.

Joel Dobson 2011

ACKNOWLEDGMENTS

Disclaimer. In over sixty years of flying, the B-52 has been revised many times. So has much of the information published in periodicals about the Goldsboro Broken Arrow of 1961. It is impossible to cover all aspects of this event, just as it is to cover all the variations of the aircraft. There may be inaccuracies, gaps, and inconsistencies, just as there may be in fifty-year-old memories. But for the purpose of this discussion, I choose to point out what I believe the aircraft was like in 1961 and the best information that is now available about the weapons and their safety features: what we thought then and now—a half century later.

Disclaimer to Disclaimer. The one exception to "what the aircraft was like in 1961" is the reference to it as BUFF (Big Ugly Fat Fellow) as opposed to BUF (Big Ugly Fellow). That one letter has created more discussion than practically any other subject on this project. BUF was the original derisive term used by fighter pilots in Vietnam who were upset by their losses in Operation Rolling Thunder; and the F was definitely not for the word fellow. In 1965 correspondents added a second F for a sanitized version: fat fellow, making the acronym BUFF. But here I must yield to the sheer weight of time: BUF was apparently used only one decade, the 1960s. BUFF has been used in the 1970s, '80s, '90s, and on.

JD

An Unusual Memorial Dinner

Billy Reeves, one of the eyewitnesses who was closest to the 1961 crash site, shared a great deal of information about Faro, North Carolina. He has been instrumental in providing contacts and stories; and his off-road, guided tour of the area was especially appreciated. Billy worked tirelessly in setting up the Memorial Dinner at the Faro Volunteer Fire Station on February 8, 2011, which was fifty years, two weeks, and one mile away from the crash. Attending were: Pilot Adam Mattocks and his wife, Anne, from Jacksonville, NC; Dr. Jack ReVelle, the explosive ordnance disposal (EOD) officer who deactivated the bombs, from Orange, California; Cliff Nelson, Web site originator; Earl Lancaster, who was assistant fire chief at the time, with his wife, Mary; Rudolph Tyndall, whose parent's house was right beside the main crash; C. T. Davis, who owned the land where both bombs landed; Brent Tyndall, who farms the land; Roy Heidicker, PhD, and historian of Fourth Fighter Wing at Seymour Johnson Air Force Base; Doc was there with his wife, Judine; Wilton Strickland, retired USAF Lt. Col. with his wife, Alice; Guy Altizer, former nuclear weapons technician at SJAFB; Andy Tulloch, son of the aircraft commander; and current members of the Faro and Eureka Volunteer Fire Stations. A meeting like that had never occurred before, and as near as we could figure, it probably would never happen again.

Through the B-52 Association, I made contact with three extremely helpful individuals:

Lieutenant Colonel Wilton Strickland, a retired B-52 radar navigator, civil engineer, and writer, was stationed at Robins AFB in Georgia and Kincheloe AFB in Michigan, where he was the wing standardization officer. That is the official who decided who was qualified to be on the front line as a SAC radar navigator in the Cold War. He was also at Seymour Johnson AFB, where he was the chief of the Bombing and Navigation Division. He was awarded three Distinguished Flying Crosses, three Meritorious Service Medals, five Air Medals, and he retired in 1981 with twenty-two years of active service. Wilton provided me with the keen insight of a professional airman and he has been a great mentor.

Mike Meager, who was a B-52 crew chief at Ramey, Anderson, and Mather Air Force Bases in the 1960s and 1970s. He was awarded the

SAC Master Crew Chief Badge in 1971. He was very helpful in my understanding of the innards of the G-model.

Pete Seberger, former BUF pilot, retired flight instructor, and organic farmer, gave assistance through a labyrinth of aircraft procedures. His learning experiences helped me understand some things about flying the B-52. He made the definition of compression stalls an explicit experience—frightening, but very explicit. Pete Seberger uses the earlier '60s BUF version, the way God intended it to be.

I have really appreciated the help and guidance of all these gentlemen throughout this project.

Crew Information

I requested the personnel records of all the crewmembers from the National Military Personnel Records Center in St. Louis. I received some information on all individuals except for Major Tulloch and Lieutenant Wilson.

Through Ancestors.com I found that Walter Scott Tulloch died on May 9, 1992, in San Diego, California. In 2010 I made contact with his widow, Betty Tulloch. She told me that he retired from the Air Force as Lieutenant Colonel Tulloch in 1967. Betty provided the Colonel's actual Pilot Individual Flight Records, his flight log covering his entire flying career. He had 6,740 hours of flying time, 458 of in it in combat. To put this in perspective, he had twice as many combat hours that I had to have in total flying time to qualify for a commercial pilot's license. Scott Tulloch's military records were sealed, possibly at the officer's request. Betty Tulloch, as next of kin, requested and received the records as per regulations. Betty shared those records with me.

A fire in 1973 damaged a large area of the Records Center in St. Louis destroying the records of some surnames, among them the officer records of Major Richards. A helpful archives technician called me with his available enlisted data. The Center has no record at all for Lieutenant Wilson apparently due to the 1973 fire at the Record Center.

The archive records showed that Adam Mattocks was from Maysville, North Carolina. I did an Internet search for any telephone numbers for that surname in that town and the very first one I tried had an address on Mattocks Road. That very fortunate lead turned out to be a relative who gladly gave me Adam's phone number. Adam Mattocks accredits his survival to one source: the prayers of all his kinfolk to God for his safety. Adam and his wife Anne are enjoying their children, their eleven grandchildren, and their five great-grandchildren in North

Carolina. He is the only known survivor of *Keep 19*. The photograph of Adam as a very young, student pilot was one of only two from that period. All other photos were lost in a house fire in the 1970s.

Other Information

Some of the information on nuclear bombs came from the book *Broken Arrow: The Declassified History of U.S. Nuclear Weapons Accidents* (2007), by Jim Oskins and Mike Maggelet, two retired experts in this field. They were both very helpful via e-mail discussions and challenged me on several points, resulting in much further research. When they did not feel comfortable with certain declassified but still sensitive data, they steered me to other available published sources. They never comment on classified material. Other information is based on the DVD *No Easy Days*, produced by Doug Keeney, and his book *15 Minutes: General Curtis LeMay and the Countdown to Nuclear Annihilation*. He is a Cold War historian, and provided me with copies of various documents, things that he obtained over the years through the Freedom of Information Act (FOIA). He searched his personal files to find a critical missing page of the history of flight for the 1961 accident. Information on actions during the in-flight emergency came from the unredacted (not blacked out) portions of the *AF Form 14*; and the *History of Flight* was provided by the archivist at Kirtland AFB, New Mexico, and Louie Alley, FOIA Manager. Hopefully at some point in the future, we will be able to obtain even the redacted portions, hopefully from Louie himself. Thanks also to Staff Sergeant Michael Thomas of the Egress section of the 372 TRS Training Squadron, SJAFB, for his detailed analysis of ejection seats and survival kits. He brought to life what it would be like to wrestle with an inflated boat, in midair, at midnight, after bailing out of an exploding B-52 bomber. Information and access to the G-model B-52 at STRATCOM HQ was provided by Ryan Hansen of the Fifty-fifth Wing Public Affairs Office, Offutt Air Force Base, Nebraska. Ryan was kind enough to escort me onto the base on his day off. STRATCOM formerly was known as Headquarters SAC. Brian York, Curator of Exhibits & Collections of the Strategic Air and Space Museum in Ashland, Nebraska, made available the extensive museum archives. Wings Over The Rockies Air & Space Museum in Denver, Colorado, provided the ejection seat graphics. Archivist Marilyn Chang was very helpful by letting me review large boxes of B-52 flight manuals and other data from the museum's reference files. The museum is on the site of the original Air Force Academy in Denver where it was first started.

I found a great deal of information in a 2005 thesis written by Scott Hardy when he was a graduate student at the East Carolina University (ECU). He lived in nearby La Grange, and he wrote his master's degree in history thesis titled: *The Broken Arrow of Camelot: An Analysis of the 1961 B-52 Crash and Loss of the Nuclear Weapon in Faro, North Carolina*. I have since met Scott who is now a minister in La Grange, North Carolina. It was the great detective work of Christine Anderson, the reference librarian at ECU, who located the only known surviving copy of the thesis and told me how to borrow it. I found the Web site ibiblio.org, which was started by four students at the University of North Carolina, Chapel Hill as part of class requirements under Professor Paul Jones. He put me in touch with Cliff Nelson, who headed up the project ten years ago. As part of the project, Cliff interviewed several interesting people such as Ralph Lapp, Daniel Ellsberg, and Chuck Hansen. Family member Jerry Barnish provided information and photographs of his cousin, Frank. Bob Shelton provided the only clear photo of a young Gene Shelton in arctic gear.

The Explosive Ordnance Disposal (EOD)

I found a very important clue in a copy of the original 1961 report by the EOD team commander. That report was in a batch of declassified documents provided by Jim Oskins. The signature on the report was that of First Lt. Jack B. ReVelle. I searched his name through Google and sent him an e-mail; he called me back immediately. And that was early on a Saturday morning on the East Coast. He was on the West Coast. I found out he lived in California, he was a well-known consultant on statistics and quality control, and is the author of over twenty books on those subjects. He was listed on his Web site as a nuclear weapons expert in the Air Force in the 1960s; that's how I found him. Jack has been exceptionally supportive and helpful in providing a first person account of the locations, recovery, and safing of the two thermonuclear devices. Goldsboro was his second Broken Arrow. The first was the 1960 Bomarc explosion and fire in storage at McGuire AFB, New Jersey. He later participated in twenty-five nuclear tests at Christmas Island and was involved in government work in Washington, DC. He is extremely knowledgeable, and I am honored to count Jack ReVelle as a friend.

Thank you, thank you very much...

Special thanks goes to my wife, Judy, who put up with me while I chased details—also for putting up with me in general for the past forty-nine years.

A very special thanks goes to Bernetiae Reed for photographing, taping, and guiding me through the fine art of recording stuff for posterity. Thanks to Lt. Col. Derek Duke, who encouraged me to keep digging; and to Jim Oskins and Mike Maggelet. Also I want to thank Jerry Smith, of the T. A. Loving Company, of Goldsboro, for information on his company that did the digging at Site Two; and historian Evan Keel.

Also, thanks to two others: Dr. Bob Claxton, for the necessary gut checks and all-round guidance and support. Support also came from Dr. John Crowder, who helped define the mysterious centerline of the Nahunta Swamp. John works in biology and environmental science. Fortunately for all of us, he is not so well-known for his work in the field of *the coefficient of retrograde phase specificity in Cholmondely's Grillage Factor.*

Prologue

If you are any good with a golf club, you could stand on Big Daddy's Road near Faro, North Carolina, and visualize an easy 140-yard golf shot hitting a certain spot in a bean field near an old cemetery. According to what some experts are now saying, that spot is ground zero of an event that might have been a true catastrophe—perhaps the largest man-made disaster in history.

On a moonlit night in 1961, a B-52 bomber disintegrated in midair twelve miles north of Goldsboro, and its two huge bombs spilled out. They were three-ton, MK-39 thermonuclear bombs. A giant one-hundred-foot-wide retardation parachute opened on the first one and it caught upright in a group of three trees, the nose just hitting the ground. But the parachute on the second bomb failed to open due to the violence of the exploding airplane, and that bomb, traveling over seven hundred miles per hour, buried itself where your golf ball would hit. The radioactive core of that bomb is still there, about 180 feet below ground level.

PART I

PART I

Chapter 1

The Crew and Their Plane

Frank Barnish was looking forward to flying the next day, Monday morning. He didn't like being cooped up in the concrete alert facility for four days and nights straight, just waiting for the Klaxon horn to go off. It was like being in jail, an underground jail at that. The facility was called the mole hole, because the bottom half of the two-story building was below ground level. If the Klaxon went off, the crews standing alert would run up the tunnels to ground level, jump in their blue station wagons or trucks, and peel out to their aircraft. Everybody would hop out and slam the doors, all except the driver. He would leave the engine running and the driver's door open for someone on the ground crew to move the vehicle out of the way of the aircraft.

There was only so much Frank could do while standing alert for SAC, the Strategic Air Command. The first day of alert wasn't so bad; there was always plenty to do. The crew would show up at six a.m., get a weather briefing, and then go out to the airplane in the truck. It was said those trucks and station wagons had a short vehicle life. The most they were ever driven was just a few hundred yards—and very hard at that. In this business seconds really did matter.

The airplanes were always cocked and ready to go, guarded twenty-four hours a day. They even had a sign posted on them that read, "Cocked." The new crew would switch baggage with the old crew, stowing their gear and briefcases in the airplane. Each crewmember's baggage included a RON kit, in the event crewmen had to *remain over night*. Crewmembers never knew where they would wind up, if for any reason the plane had to divert. The pilots would then do the preflight walk-around inspection with the crew chief, looking for leaks and checking fluid levels. Frank went to the upper deck and checked out his guns. Even though the guns were over a hundred feet away in the tail, Frank's station was in the front of the airplane, a situation that suited Frank just fine. Soon, the two navigators would set up a stepladder to peer inside the bombs hanging in the bomb bays.

After preflight it was back to the alert facility for breakfast, and then briefings followed by more briefings. The two navigators would go off to the Wing target vault, for DITR study. That was Defense Intelligence Target Reconnaissance. They would look at aerial photos of their targets. Frank didn't know how good those spy cameras were, but sometimes the navigators would discuss the scores at Russian soccer games. At some point, around the third day, the boredom would set in for just about everybody on the crew. Standing alert was boring. It was the days off alert when the real flying happened. Long, exhausting, full days of twenty-four-hour flying, but it wasn't like sitting in that concrete mole hole.

The six-man crew had reached the end of the four day alert period and had finished all the items of the mission briefing for the next day's flight. Frank could go home for one night, then go out and fly for twenty-five hours, and then have a day off. He usually liked flying, especially with this crew. They were called Readiness Crew R-10, of the 4241st Strategic Wing at Seymour Johnson Air Force Base, Goldsboro, North Carolina. Frank was Francis R. E. Barnish, thirty-five-years-old, of Greenfield, Massachusetts, and he was the gunner, a technical sergeant in the US Air Force, and the only enlisted man on Readiness Crew R-10.

They would fly the Boeing B-52 Stratofortress, the eight-engine jet bomber nicknamed the BUFF, (an acronym politely translated to *Big Ugly Fat Fellow*). They would fly a loop route near the US East Coast on a so-called training mission, but everyone in the Wing knew that the SAC Commander-In-Chief General Thomas Power had announced publicly just a few days earlier that a new program called Airborne Alert had begun. There would be at least twelve bombers in the air at all times, the exact number would be classified. Also classified, but not announced, were the specific long-range mission routes, called Chrome Dome, which would involve flying over Greenland, Canada, and the around the Mediterranean. Crews from Seymour Johnson flew the Southern, or Mediterranean route. That week's training mission was to prove they were ready to go to war.

Operation Chrome Dome would continue for seven more years, always ready to carry the fire to the Russians. The fire that Crew R-10 would carry that Monday morning was in the form of two MK-39 thermonuclear weapons— hydrogen bombs. Combined, these two fully armed special weapons had the destructive power five hundred times that of the Hiroshima bomb, used seventeen years before.

The B-52 was, and still is, a workhorse of the United States Air Force bomber fleet. It has served in many engagements—the Cold War, Vietnam, Iraq, Afghanistan—even involved in space programs for NASA by hauling X-15s to the edge of space. Based on longevity alone, it is probably the most successful and versatile military aircraft ever designed. Compared to the prop driven B-29, we think of the B-52 jet bomber as relatively modern, but some people may find it curious that the B-29 is only ten years older than the B-52. The B-29 first flew in 1942; the B-52's first flight was on April 15, 1952. That was more than a half-century ago, and the B-52 will probably still fly for decades more. Today's B-52 is frequently twice as old as the airmen who service it. Lieutenant Chuck Lutter, a B-52 pilot, recently said in an interview about the Air Force, "It may not be your father's Air Force, but it could be his airplane. In my case, it is." His father flew in the exact same B-52 aircraft in Vietnam, the same "tail number."

It is not a graceful aircraft on the ground. It is huge. When a group of fat, gray B-52s move at maximum taxi speed from the alert pad to the active runway, they lumber from side to side because of their heaviness and width. Due to their enormous size, it appears that they move very slowly and awkwardly. This is called the *elephant walk*. After a soaking rain, jets of water will shoot up from the expansion joints of the concrete taxiways as the heavy bombers pass by.

For the B-52 to be as big as it is, the crewmembers sit in a relatively small portion: the front, or sharp end. Depending on the model, the aircraft is 160 feet long and the wingspan is about 185 feet across. It weighs close to a half million pounds at takeoff—488,000 pounds.

The Boeing B-52 Stratofortress—The BUFF.
Image courtesy of the USAF

The B-52 could fly at 50,000 feet, at Mach 0.86, about 650 miles per hour, and carry up to 70,000 pounds of bombs—and do it all day and all night in a perpetual giant loop. At the end of the assigned tour, that BUFF would be replaced by another BUFF, followed by another, and another. It was always on full airborne alert in the 1960s, refueled in midair, always ready for thermonuclear war. There were between six and thirteen B-52s in the air at any time during this period. At the height of the Cold War, the Strategic Air Command flew the B-52s an incredible 47,168 hours for the month of October 1962. Airborne alert operated at highest strength during the Cuban Missile Crisis with approximately sixty-five bombers in the air and "target effective" at any given time. When SAC was at its peak, it had 2,921 bombers and tankers, and 15,468 nuclear bombs, aimed at 3,729 targets, with the equivalent megatonnage of 13 Hiroshima's per target. The Soviets, by contrast, had 1,060 bombs at that time. SAC was on ground alert for 35 years, ready to launch on 15-minutes notice to strike targets in the Soviet Union with nuclear weapons. That was a far cry from 1945, at the end of World War II, when the United States was the sole nuclear power, but without a single operational nuclear weapon. We had just used them all on Japan.

In the 1960s, the prime weapons carriers of SAC were the B-47 and the B-52. The B-47 would be dropped from SAC bomber inventory, the B-58 Hustler would be added, then dropped after a spectacular but brief ten year service, but the B-52 BUFF was destined to live on for decades.

It had already been determined that the Soviets would have the ability to launch intercontinental ballistic missiles (ICBMs) against America in a surprise attack that would result in massive destruction. It was also determined that the US would have only fifteen minutes of advance warning. That made it essential to have the ability to launch the bomber fleet within that time period to both act as a deterrent and to save a portion of the fleet—to get aircraft safely away from SAC bases that were sure to be targets. The bombers would have to be completely ready to go, fueled up, weapons aboard, fully trained crews available, and standing ready. The ground alert was born. It would be enormously expensive, both in treasure and manpower. The amount of force necessary to retaliate was calculated to be a minimum of one-third of its 550 bombers and 350 tankers. That is what it would take in 1961 to survive to fight the nuclear fight,—the goal set by SAC at the time Crew R-10 was getting ready to fly.

The fifteen-minute launch window for a SAC wing was in reality much shorter. A typical wing at that time was made up of forty-five bombers and thirty tankers. To get one-third off the ground within fifteen minutes meant that the first of the fifteen bombers and ten tankers would have to be *wheels up* in about seven minutes. To meet that goal required an enormous investment, an estimated capital outlay of 8.5 billion dollars, bigger than the largest industrial corporation in the world at that time: Standard Oil of New Jersey.

Every man on a SAC bomber crew in the 1960s was aware of something that very few modern warriors ever had to face. If they went off to war—the war they were trained to fight—there was a very good chance it would be their families, not them, that would pay the ultimate price. If the worst-case scenario came and they had to launch a nuclear strike against the Soviet Union, they knew their families would be at extreme risk. They might return safely from their mission to find out their families were the casualties of a nuclear counterstrike.

That day started out warm for January at Seymour Johnson Air Force Base in Goldsboro, North Carolina. But during the day it turned windy and chilly, and by late night a cold front would come through in force. The 4241st Strategic Wing was a *tenant* unit on a Tactical Air Command Base. Three days before, our country had inaugurated a new president, John F. Kennedy, and we were at the height of the Cold War. He had said in his inauguration address, "We will pay any price, bear any burden, meet any hardship, support any friend, oppose any foe, in order to assure the survival and the success of liberty."

It was Monday, January 23, 1961.

The Men on *The Sharp End*

The pilot of Alert Crew R-10 was Air Force Major Walter Scott Tulloch, forty-five-years-old, of San Diego, California. On the day Pearl Harbor was attacked, he was a twenty-five-year-old clerk with a high school education and a private pilot's license. Within three days he was enlisted in the Army Air Corps as an aviation cadet. Six months after that, he earned his Army Air Corps pilot wings, a very fast track. In World War II, he flew thirty-one combat missions from the Northern Mariana Islands over Japan in B-29s. By 1961 he was a senior, or command pilot in the Strategic Air Command, had logged almost six thousand flying hours, and had been a pilot for nineteen years. He was at the pinnacle of what SAC wanted: a highly trained, professional pilot. He had flown every bomber the Air Force had in inventory at that time, from B-17s to B-36s to the B-52.

His copilot, flying *right seat* was Captain Richard Rardin, thirty-three-years-old,' from San Antonio, Texas. He enlisted as a private as soon as he was eighteen-years-old, in his home state of Ohio. After four years of enlisted service, he was commissioned in 1950, and he became a pilot in 1952. He had been a fighter pilot and test pilot, and had survived three flameouts in test aircraft. Captain Rardin was also a World War II veteran, a tall, gray-haired, thirty-year-old. He didn't talk much about the war. The way he saw it, his job, with that of his boss, was to keep them out of the rocks.

Major Walter Scott Tulloch,
Aircraft Commander, Keep 19.
Image courtesy Betty Tulloch

Dick Rardin, Copilot, Captain.
Photo not dated, probably from
the 1980s, as Lieutenant Colonel.
Image courtesy of the USAF

The electronic warfare officer, or EW, was First Lieutenant Bill Wilson, age twenty-seven, of Somerville, New Jersey. He sat ten feet behind the copilot, facing aft; his job was to identify and use various countermeasures against incoming missiles, whether they were guided by radar, optically, or infrared. His was a new flying profession. Pilots and navigators have always been pilots and navigators, and gunners have always been gunners. But when the Air Force first started the Electronic Countermeasures Program, the other crewmembers didn't even know what to call them: EWOs, EWs, ECMs, or what? They even spoke their own language, which sounded like gibberish when they congregated together at the Officer's Club. They wore the wings of the navigator rating, and sat facing backward in the far dark corner of the B-52 upper deck, surrounded by their black boxes. Up until the G-model B-52 they sat back there by themselves. The EW's specialty group of veterans would later be known as the Old Crows, as in wise old birds. Bill Wilson's job was to defend his aircraft by jamming, decoying, and confusing enemy missiles or radar, for the EW's fight was a war with invisible electronic impulses.

To Lieutenant Wilson's right sat the gunner. He fought with very traditional bullets: .50 caliber shells. Technical Sergeant Frank Barnish sat in the fourth ejection seat on the top deck, also facing aft, where he watched radar and TV monitors. He used the screens to remotely control his four .50 caliber machine guns back in the tail, capable of firing twenty-four hundred rounds a minute. Frank was the only enlisted man aboard and one of a rare breed—the flying sergeant. In World War II, he had been shot down over Germany and bailed out of his B-24 bomber. That was on the ill-fated Kassel Mission of World War II and he was the turret gunner on the bomber *Our Gal*. It was shot out of the sky along with twenty-four other aircraft in just three minutes on September 27, 1944. He was nineteen-years-old then, and became a prisoner of war in central Germany. After the war, he spent a few years in the civilian world as an auto mechanic, but came back into the Air Force as a gunner in the Strategic Air Command.

Lieutenant Bill Wilson,
Electronic Warfare Officer. 1961.
Image courtesy of the USAF

Sergeant Frank Barnish,
Gunner. Photo taken early
World War II, around 1943.
Image courtesy of Jerry Barnish

BUFF gunners on the G-model said that they had a good deal because previous models of the B-52 had the tail gunner physically located back in the tail, just like some World War II bombers. Just getting into that cramped *office* way back in the earlier models was different from the rest of the crew. The tail gunner usually did not climb into the aircraft at the belly hatch like everyone else, if he wanted to avoid a very long crawl through the bomb bay dragging his parachute and other gear. Instead, he used a ground maintenance stand and entered through a hatch up high on the side of the rear fuselage, under the right horizontal stabilizer. If the ground stand was not available, he could crawl in through the aft wheel well. Also, the tail gunners were isolated on the older B-52s. Being way out back, away from the wing, made for a very rough ride during turbulence. But the worse thing was that if a bail out command came, the section containing the entire big gun assembly would be dropped—cut completely loose from the airplane—right there in front of the gunner. He would then release his seat belt and take a tumbling dive through this new opening. Then it was up to him to hand-deploy his parachute.

The relocation of the gunner from the tail section to a much safer ejection seat behind the pilot greatly improved the morale of the gunners of the G-model B-52. It even had a cup warmer and small oven. Sergeant Barnish was happy to have his ejection seat up front with the rest of the crew.

These two fellow crewmen, EW and 'Guns,' the only ones who rode around the world backward, formed a very small fraternity of two. The EWs and gunners had a shoulder patch showing a gruff bulldog firing a machine gun alongside a crafty-looking black bird. The other men frequently kidded them, asking if the shoulder patch was on backward just because of their weird seating arrangement in the aircraft.

Two more ejection seats were on the lower deck. Major Eugene Shelton, forty-one-years-old, of San Antonio, Texas, the radar navigator (RN), sat in the left seat facing forward. He had a wife named Rusty, three sons, and a daughter. The other seat was for the navigator (NAV), Captain Paul Brown, thirty-seven-years-old, of Beardstown, Illinois. He had survived two crashes in World War II. These men had answered the call back when it was the Army Air Corps. They were side by side down on the lower deck in what they called *The Hole*. It was a dark area, only a few feet from back to front, twelve feet wide, and not enough room to stand up. No windows. They needed darkness to stare at the screens.

Only the two pilots on the upper deck could see outside the aircraft.

Major Gene Shelton,
Radar Navigator.
Photo probably from 1943.
Image courtesy of the
Shelton Family

Captain Paul Brown,
Navigator. (1961)
Image courtesy of the
USAF

Major Shelton's job as radar navigator is somewhat of a misnomer because this officer did much more than navigate by radar. He was also much more than the bombardier. The RN is responsible for the arming, aiming, and releasing of the weapons or bombs. A better name would be radar navigator/bombardier since he performed jobs that were three separate crew positions on the earlier bombers. The exclusive reason for the B-52 at that time, as the deterrent to nuclear war, lies at Major Shelton's left hand: the Weapons Monitor and Control Panel for each of the two nuclear bombs. This electrical panel is only five inches by eight inches in physical size, but its potency was enormous. On the flat, metal panel was a round wafer switch, the DCU/9A, held in the SAFE position with a knobbed pin secured by a breakable copper wire. It is very difficult to actuate, designed that way for a very good purpose. It takes both hands: break the safety wire, unscrew the knobbed release pin with your right hand, and pull it straight out toward you a fraction of an inch while turning it to the right. It is the only control device—out of about three hundred devices spread over eighty separate panels—that requires both hands to operate. While holding the release pin out with the right hand, the RN would turn the round wafer part with his left hand. That would send a 28-volt DC electrical current to the MC-772 Arm/Safe Switch, located inside the back end of the selected thermonuclear bomb hanging in the bomb bay. The bomb was carefully inspected on every preflight inspection. A retired radar navigator once told me, "On your preflight, you could look through a little window in the bomb to inspect the Arm/Safe Switch and see either a green S (for SAFE) or a red A (for ARM). If you saw the red A, somebody had really screwed up, and this would be a good time to get excited."

Radar bombing was a skill in itself. Practice targets known as *show* targets would be identified by radar returns from known large, stationary objects, like bridges or buildings. When missile silos went underground, with no discernible structures, a new skill set was devised: offset bombing. By using the known distances and known direction from *show* targets, the hidden *no show* targets would be offset, and identified on the RN's radar. In practice bomb runs on America's prairies it would appear they were bombing an empty spot on the windswept plains, but they would know if they hit the practice *no show* site. It was estimated that 90 percent of all Soviet targets were *no show*.

SAC crews practiced bombing the same practice radar bombing sites in the US so often that they became too well-known, so SAC invented the *RBS Express*. The radar bombing targets were put in sealed boxcars of three trains traveling around three parts of the country. The sealed units would transmit electronic images identifying them as targets. The purpose was to eliminate crew familiarity with permanent sites.

On an actual bomb run there were many more tasks for the RN to do before the arming of the bomb: navigate, avoid detection, find the target, etc. On the final bomb run the Radar Navigator would allow his computers to take over control of the aircraft: the heading, when to release, even when to open and close the bomb bay doors. All based on the data he carefully entered before and during the flight. The nuclear bombing checklist also included other details to be read off and complied with such as: the pilots closing their thermal curtains to prevent flash blindness; going to combat cabin pressurization, in case the hull was breached; reminding the crew to set their personal locator beacon lanyards to activate and start sending impulses in case their parachute was engaged—this may not apply on all missions—sometimes you didn't want people to know where you were; and a number of other items, such as seals to break, and circuits to engage.

Thermonuclear bombs were known as special weapons. In order for one to be dropped, a complex series of steps had to occur, all in exactly the right order. An eight-letter Go Code had to be received by radio, copied with a grease pencil on a plastic-covered form, then decoded independently by three people: the EW, the Navigator, and the Radar Navigator. All three had to agree. The first four letters referred to a page in a code book, and the second four letters on that page had to match the color code and characters of execution tickets kept in a heavy, double-locked safe that two men had carried aboard and then locked down. The aircraft commander and the navigator each unlocked the safe when the Emergency War Order called for it.

They would follow a lengthy checklist, involving a verbal statement by one crewmember, answered by another. Any deviation, any anomaly, could interrupt the process, or possibly even deactivate the weapon and abort the mission. If you made an error in the checklist, you were only allowed so many tries, then the weapon disabled itself. Then you had some explaining to do at mission debriefing back at the base.

As part of his *Checklist, Bomb Drop, (Nuclear)*, the electronic warfare officer situated on the upper deck would reach down beside his right foot and pull out a cable that physically removed a locking pin from the bomb's mounting rack in the bomb bay. The pilot would then "vote" by activating his Bomb Readiness Switch located by his left elbow. He did not, contrary to some movies, have the ability to either arm or drop the bombs. He approved, but did not arm or release.

The radar navigator downstairs would break the copper wire on his bomb control DCU/9A. He would then take a big breath, maybe say a prayer, and pull the pin while turning the knob—the last human action to set in motion the opening of Pandora's Box. This may happen hundreds of miles away from the target.

If all equipment was working well, the aircraft's computers would determine the aircraft's heading, and the instant to release the bomb, based on his input. The RN would continue to monitor, refining the crosshairs, watching over his minions. He also had the ability to stop the process entirely. One way was by yanking a handle to pull out the Release Circuits Disconnect (RCD), a large electrical plug, or he could override the system and manually drop the weapon, by pulling an overhead D-ring, the special weapons release cable.

Stainless steel pins would release the U-2 hook on the big bicycle chain holding up the bomb.

The armed bomb would drop.

Three officers, the pilot, the electronic warfare officer, and the radar navigator, are located in three different areas of the aircraft, areas that are the most physically distant from each other: two were on the upper deck, one on the lower. Each would have to perform a physical task in the planned, deliberate, and exact sequence to release a nuclear weapon. That was the intent of SAC's Human Reliability Program, a part of which was the so-called *two-man* policy. In the BUFF's case, it was actually three-man. That policy would ensure that no single person, at any time, would be alone with a nuclear weapon, and that every member of the team was equally familiar with the task at hand to know when proper procedures were followed. The policy required the conscious decision of more than one knowledgeable crewmember, men in that plane, at that time, to physically set the circuitry to start the process of an armed weapon drop. That effectively removed the possibility of a rogue crewman taking over a SAC aircraft and dropping the bomb single-handedly.

Air Force SAC Missile programs, such as the Titan and Minuteman, would have the same policy. The two Missile Launch Officers had different keys to insert in different switches, located physically apart, and turned at the same instant. In some units, the keys of the missile commander and the deputy commander were on big metal rings worn around their necks. At change of tour, a little ceremony was held in the underground silo signifying the transfer of control of the missile. It involved the old and new crews facing each other, a countdown, and the flipping of the big key ring from each man's neck to the other. Another part of the Human Reliability Program was the arming of the missile launch officers with side arms. It was rumored, hopefully in jest, that the pistols were not just for intruders breaking into the underground missile silo; if the other guy started acting crazy or you thought he was trying somehow to launch a missile by himself, shoot him.

A major complaint from BUFF crews was about the comfort level of the ejection seats, or rather, the lack of comfort. Many marveled at how it was possible to spend millions of dollars to perfect an ejection seat that is adjustable six ways and still is not able to make it to a bearable sitting position. You could not adjust the seat too frequently because you had to let the electric seat motors rest to avoid overheating. You could not bring a seat cushion from home (although some did), because "the chance of vertebral injury is increased considerably by sitting on too thick a compressible mass." You just had to sit there, for twenty-four hours or so, on those chute straps that were part of the complex system that would "save your sorry butt during an ejection."

For the B-52 to be as big as it is, the amount of room for the occupants is extremely small. For other than the pilots, it is comparable to taking a very long trip in a very small car without windows. Another way is to visualize sitting in front of a computer screen for twenty-four hours, which is inside an aluminum aircraft cargo container, the kind that holds luggage. Now load it in a cargo aircraft and fly it to Spain and back, all the while tilting, shaking, dropping, and climbing. It was not quite as bad as the way one of the early Gemini astronauts described the two person NASA orbital space flight: "Both of you put on space suits, then get in a Volkswagen. One of you carries a television set on your lap for eight days. That's it."

There were other expressions of opinion. In the center of each steering yoke for the pilot and copilot was a circle with a stylized *Boeing B-52*. At the bottom of the black yoke was printed, in white, *STRATOFORTRESS*. At least one joker, with too much time on autopilot, scratched out seven of those letters, and changed the second O to an A, thus christening his airplane *RAT FART*.

Later, in the Vietnam era, this sense of dark humor continued. At every SAC installation was a sign with the SAC emblem: a mailed fist holding lightning bolts and an olive branch with the phrase, "Peace Is Our Profession." Sometimes someone would add, "War Is Just Our Hobby."

In spite of all the discomfort and stress of flying the B-52, there was still the thrill of the hunt and the need for speed that all pilots know. Here is the way a former pilot with the Strategic Air Command described it to historian Doug Keeney: "After takeoff, we'd go get gas and then we'd fly to out first waypoint, our PCTAP—the Positive Control Turn Around Point. If we were executed, that is, if we were told to proceed, we'd go as far as the H-Hour Control Line. If we got the proper codes, at our Start Descent point, we'd push over the nose. At our Terrain Avoidance Point we'd be flying low level inbound to our target, maybe two hours out, as low to the ground as our sortie required. We were already low level. The Soviet fighters couldn't see us down low. When we got to our Initial Point, which was where we'd start the bomb run, we'd go another four, five minutes then pop the bomb bay doors at ten seconds, pull the nose up at five seconds, release our weapon, then push it over and get back down. We're going 390 knots with our hair on fire."

SAC created special routes across the US countryside for this low-level training. They were called *Oil Burner* routes, and were sometimes as long as five hundred miles. They name came from the streams of black smoke pouring out of the B-52 as it flew at near treetop level.

I experienced one of these Oil Burner exercises, from the ground level. I was using the small airport at Post, Texas, in 1977, working on my instrument rating. I had finished off with some touch-and-go landings, and was driving home and decided to stop and enjoy the West Texas sunset with a cold 'Texas longneck.' It was utterly quiet except for the birds, miles away from civilization. The fading light was incredible, a perfect evening along the rolling hills below the caprock of the high plains.

A low rumble shook the ground. I turned around to find the source, when suddenly, from out of nowhere, the biggest, loudest, meanest looking airplane in the world rose out of the low hills just to the north, landing lights on, black smoke pouring out, and screamed right over my head; or rather, my butt, because I had hit the deck. The ground was shaking, dust was flying, and small stones levitated. The noise was incredible. The BUFF looked like it was flying about fifty feet off the ground. It had to be at least two hundred feet or so, but it sure looked, felt, and smelled like fifty or less.

I later checked the NOTAMs (Notices To Airmen) and found that I was right at the exit end of an Oil Burner route that began in Oklahoma.

There are several phrases for describing flying speed, such as "going 390 knots with our hair on fire." Another is, "Taking off like God's ape, late for work." I have no idea where that came from.

The B-52 on takeoff is quite impressive. As an additive to the fuel, some models including the G, could use up to ten thousand pounds of water depending on gross weight and temperature, in the first two minutes of takeoff. This water injection would give a boost of around 15 percent in takeoff power. It would also contribute to the black smoke spewing out because almost four times the amount of water as fuel was pouring into the engines en masse. If the water was not used up on takeoff, it had to be dumped before reaching altitude because the water would freeze there.

The BUFF's crew navigator (NAV) is primarily responsible for the aircraft's position. He must get the aircraft and the bomb close enough to the target to allow the RN to place the bomb on target at the right time. TOT (Time On Target) was a critical event. One reason: there was a policy of multiple strikes on the same target, and you didn't want to be over the target when some other SAC bomber ahead of you happened to be early or late. That was the reason for the computer-generated master timeline for all bombers, to insure the other aircraft would be safe from other SAC bombs in going to, from, and at the target area. Several crewmembers wondered what they would do if they got to the target and it already had a mushroom shaped cloud over it. Would they drop another one into the fire or go to the alternate target?

Most SAC crews could agree on one thing: the navigator was the hardest-working man on the airplane, always figuring and rechecking. Captain Brown had to be very proficient and extremely accurate in several types of difficult long-range navigation: celestial, pressure pattern, grid navigation in the Arctic, dead reckoning, and radar navigation at very low altitude. Pressure pattern navigation was part art, part science. It proved that the shortest distance between two points is not necessarily a straight line—knowing where the atmospheric highs and lows were, or going to be, and how to best utilize current and future winds associated with them often was more important. It was sort of like windsurfing, where the surfboard has an attached sail. In this case however, the surfboard weighs about a half million pounds and carried several buckets of hell.

These six men made up a new configuration called the battle-station concept of the B-52G, placing the defensive crew (the EW and gunner) facing aft on the upper deck, and the offensive team (the two crew navigation system operators), in the Hole on the lower deck facing forward. The flight crew, the pilot and copilot, were side-by-side on the flight deck. Surprisingly, a very early prototype of the B-52 actually had the pilot and copilot sitting in tandem, one behind the other. General Curtis LeMay reportedly told Boeing during the development phase, "Change it. Put the pilots side by side and I'll buy a bunch of the damn things."

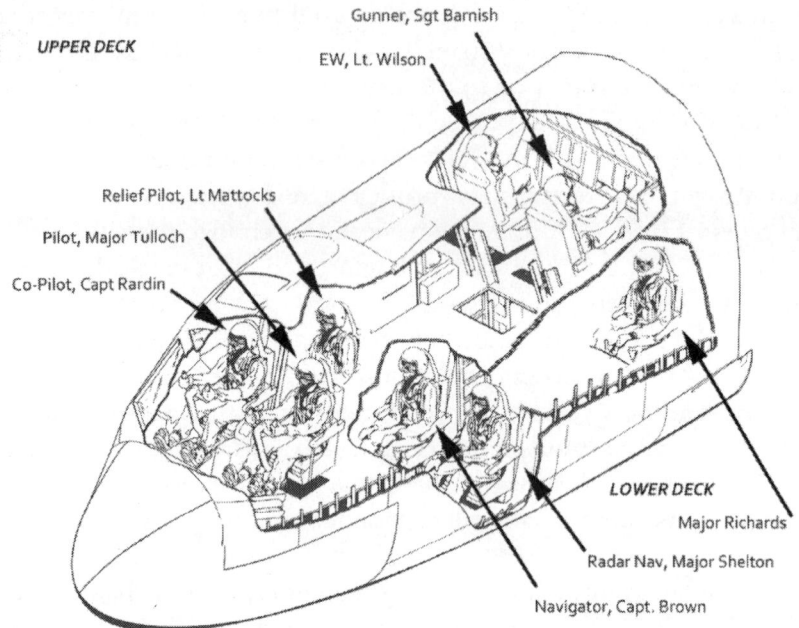

Crew Positions, Keep 19.
Image courtesy USAF, modified by author.

The G-model B-52 had eliminated the ailerons, the primary wing control surfaces traditionally used on most aircraft. Wing control was now handled by a series of spoilers on the top of each wing, seven per wing. These were metal flight control surfaces, each about three feet long, making a total of about twenty-five feet of controls along the trailing edge of the wing, just above the outboard flap. The spoilers on each wing worked in two groups: one group of four spoilers outboard as one interconnected group, and the other three inboard as a group. They were hinged at the forward edge and the trailing edge lifted sixty degrees for spoilers and fifty degrees for air brakes. Hydraulic powered pistons activated them. Spoilers were very distinctive in appearance, with long flat "fingers" off the trailing edge. The fingers had gaps between them and did a great job of *spoiling* the linear air flow over the wing. When not in use, the spoilers, with their fingers, lay down flat against the wing surface.

The more traditional ailerons work by increasing lift under one wing to raise it, and at the same time spoiling lift on the opposite wing to lower it. Spoilers work by merely creating drag and spoiling lift on one wing at a time, causing that wing to drop and forcing the other wing to rise. B-52s before the G-model had both ailerons and spoilers, but the G-, and the later H-model, had only the spoilers. Spoilers were speed brakes when used together on both wings at the same time. Some B-52 pilots were critical of spoilers, and most preferred the instant feedback response of ailerons. Spoilers also increased the tendency of the G-model to go into a frightening gyration called a Dutch roll, a problem with all large, swept wing aircraft. When a pilot initiated a turn, the spoilers caused a slight buffet, and the nose would pitch up, which was particularly troubling during the delicate aerial refueling process.

Refueling was delicate enough even without the strain of fighting skittish controls. In a fighter plane, it was said if you think about a turn, you turn. In a B-52, you turn, and a while later, the airplane agrees. Refueling was exhausting for the pilots wrestling with "the beast" below and behind the refueling tanker. At the rendezvous point, after the bomber found and moved in behind the tanker, the boom operator used a series of signal lights on the tanker's belly to help the receiving pilot with his relative approach speed and to find the proper staging location. When the bomber was in the right spot, a few feet below the boom tip, the lights on the tanker's belly turned green, and the bomber pilot held that station while the boomer *flew* the probe, using its small wings, into the four-inch-wide fuel receptacle. Once connected, it took from thirty minutes to an hour to complete the fuel transfer. Whoever flew the bomber used his own references, for example, if he could see the refueler's face in a certain corner of an overhead window, he was in the right spot. The limits of the refueling box were 20° up, 40° down, and 10° on either side. Exceed the limits and you heard the urgent words over the radio, "Breakaway-breakaway-breakaway!" as the probe was quickly withdrawn and raised. Either the boom operator or the receiver pilot could disengage. You fell back, regrouped, and the line-up process started all over again. The receiving pilot was usually drenched in sweat by the end of the transfer of fuel.

Pilots relied on the powered trim controls, which permitted continuous adjustments of nose up and down as well as aircraft heading by changing small tabs on the wings and tail. Trim was increased or decreased by small switches on the pilots' steering yoke or the larger knobbed wheel on the center console, and was constantly fine-tuned during flight. Making very small, continuous adjustments on the trim controls was the secret to making any good pilot look better. It also helped relieve some of the stress in manhandling the airplane.

Colonel Walter J. Boyne, who was an Air Force captain when he first encountered the B-52, gave a comment about spoilers in his short description of what it was like to fly the BUFF: "The control surfaces were small so you used trim a lot . . . It responded to more than one gust variation at a time and hence was never in synch. The spoilers took some getting used to. It wasn't like having conventional aileron control . . . When you took off, the wings flew before the fuselage, so the flight surfaces had to be used while the wheels were still on the ground. Also, the crosswind landing gear [which could be turned up to 20° in either direction to counteract crosswinds up to 43 knots] took some getting used to. While landing, you could be looking out the side window to see the runway ahead."

The Extras

That day in 1961, using the instructor jump seat behind and between the pilot and copilot, sat First Lieutenant Adam Mattocks. The only African-American of Crew R-10 that day, he was there as a fully qualified third pilot, a relief pilot. The third pilot was an essential member on long missions; one reason was because of the spoilers, the new change that made the job of flying the G-model more physically exhausting, especially during refueling operations. His seat was not an ejection seat, but it was right behind and between the two pilots. The seat position was called the IP, for Instructor Pilot. His job was to fly the airplane whenever either the pilot or copilot needed a break from the long hours at the controls. He would then take over and whomever he replaced could stretch out for a few minutes on the *observer's position*, which was really just a pad unrolled on the floor right behind the IP seat in this airplane.

Lieutenant Mattocks was twenty-seven-years-old and from nearby Maysville, North Carolina. He first trained as a F-86 fighter pilot and was assigned to a squadron in Arizona. But his entire fighter squadron had been reassigned to SAC to fill much-needed bomber pilot vacancies. That was certainly not a well-liked decision by the fighter pilots, moving from the single seat "fast burners" to flying a "bus." General LeMay didn't help relations between fighter pilots and bomber pilots when he said, "Flying fighters is fun. Flying bombers is important."

Adam had assignments and flight schools in Georgia, Maine, Arizona, and North Carolina. When he was transferred from the F-86, he asked for the Seymour Johnson assignment to be near his kinfolk. He was a native of Onslow County, North Carolina, and was the youngest of seven children, and the first in his family to go to college. His father talked to the rest of his brothers and sisters, and together they worked hard to send Adam to North Carolina A&T State University in Greensboro. Adam knew his wife, Anne, in college, but he couldn't date much because he was studying so hard. He studied premed; he wanted to be a doctor. He was commissioned an Air Force second lieutenant through ROTC and went off to Florida for flight training. Other young black officers told him they doubted that the Air Force would allow a black man to fly jets.

There were times when Adam Mattocks was the only African-American officer on base, and this was during the 1960s, so he did experience discrimination on some assignments. One time he and Anne had saved to buy a nice car, a 1958 white Cadillac, and one of the other officers made a crack about how he was able to afford it. "I don't spend all my money at the Officer's Club bar," was the reply. Adam always paid his club dues; he just didn't eat there frequently.

Adam believed a nearby high-ranking officer somehow overheard his comment about the Officer's Club and misinterpreted it—as if Adam didn't support the Club. That's the only reason he could figure out for getting only a *satisfactory* on his next efficiency report. For SAC flight-rated officers, getting a much higher *outstanding* or *exceptional* rating was expected. Getting the lower satisfactory mark was a real downgrade in the world of SAC-speak. Adam tried to fight it, and needed someone to help him. He asked Major Scott Tulloch, who got him assigned as the extra pilot for his crew, and gave him up-close-and-personal flight training. More importantly, he was a friend with the gold leaves of a major, a field-grade officer. The dip in Adam's performance rating soon climbed back to the top of the Officer Efficiency Reports.

Reassignment to different bases around the country meant a fast relocation move for Adam, but it could be a slow car or bus trip for Anne and the kids. Traveling alone cross-country with children was especially difficult, according to Anne. She had to carry food for three or four days in case she couldn't find a restaurant to let them eat; to sleep in the car if she couldn't find a hotel to let them stay. Somehow, someone always watched over her and the children. Once, they had to sleep in the car beside a riverbank, and a policeman told them he would check on them during the night and watch out for them. Another time, traveling by bus to catch up with a new Air Force assignment, a child became sick, and needed juice and medicine. A pharmacist turned her away. When the driver of the bus inquired, she told him of her concerns, and the next thing she knew the driver brought her the needed medicine. Over the years, Anne kept a book of the people all over the country who took her and the children in for an overnight stay, or sometimes much longer. She has stayed in touch with many of them throughout the years. She still visits with a lady who is over eighty-years-old. When they moved to Arizona, for Adam's assignment there, she lived with a black cowboy and his Indian wife. She wondered why it would take the base commander to have to order people to treat her family appropriately, especially since they were all there serving their country.

Major Eugene Richards, forty-two-years-old, of Toccoa, Georgia, was also in a jump seat, this one on the lower deck. He was on the staff at wing headquarters, and was the wing electronic warfare officer, responsible for all EW training. As such, he was not required to fly as a crewmember on a regular basis, but as a rated flying officer, he was required to stay current and fly each month. That's why he was flying that day, to help the defense team smooth out their operation and to qualify for his monthly flight pay of one hundred dollars by riding along. He had to accomplish and record the flight time before the end of the month and that day was the twenty-third. He was one of the most popular officers in Wing and very qualified. He and his wife, Sue, owned a motel, the El Rancho, on the Wilson Highway just north of Goldsboro. That's where they lived. It was not uncommon for SAC officers and sergeants to make local business investments; they had to plan for retirement.

These two men, Lieutenant Mattocks and Major Richards, were the two 'extras,' on this crew.

If there was such a thing as a seating priority on this flight, Major Richards had the least desirable, the equivalent of steerage. In a cramped spot at the back of 'The Hole' on the lower deck, his seat was an uncomfortable, nonadjustable, fold-away panel with seat belts and a headphone jack. This seat station was officially known as the IN, for instructor navigator. The backrest was a thin cushion fastened to a pressurized access door. Behind that locked door was the forward wheel well; behind that was the forward bomb bay, followed by the aft bomb bay. The fold-up, orange-colored, metal grid called the *egg crate* sat at his feet—it was a grating that protected the fold-up stairway mechanism of the crew access hatch. That was the hinged hatch in the bottom of the aircraft that served as the front door: the portal through which all crewmembers, including the gunner, on the G-model entered. Major Richards did not have much of a view from his seat, only the back of the two navigators' ejection seats. To his right and left were equipment bulkheads, and in front of him to the right was the yellow ladder to the upper deck. That's where the chemical toilet was located, just at the top of the ladder, along with a cloth privacy screen. Immediately to his left was the crew urinal canister. Some *ride-along's* who were assigned to this location on the lower deck referred to it as "the men's room."

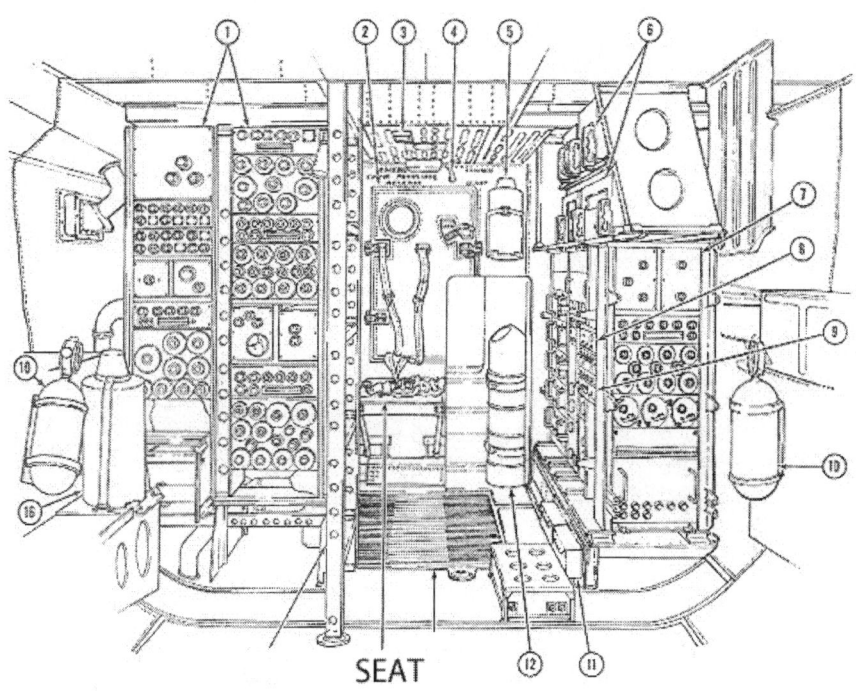

Major Richards' Seat at Aft Navigator Instructor's Position.
His backrest was the access door to the forward wheel well.
Image courtesy USAF.

B-52 H-model with Landing Gear Coming Down. Note rotation of bogies, two wheels each. Image courtesy USAF.

Chapter 2

The Mission

Readiness Crew R-10 had been on four days of alert duty which required them to live together in a dormitory-like building near their waiting and cocked aircraft, Number 58-187, ready to fly at a moment's notice. They had a briefing on the afternoon of Sunday, January 22, for a Coverall mission in accordance with Eighth Air Force Order 20-31. It would be a twenty-five-hour, non-stop flight involving two heavyweight air refuelings. It was technically called a training mission since they would not be flying the new Southern Chrome Dome looping route around the eastern end of the Atlantic and over the Mediterranean, but they would still be fully *bombed up* and ready to go to war the next morning. The route was named Southern because it began in the southern United States. Others were Northern, from Michigan, and Western, from the northwest US. There was also the Thule Monitor, which circled around and around Thule, Greenland. Chrome Dome routes would funnel one B-52 after another, a constant stream of bombers, spaced out for refueling, into a holding pattern.

That's where they would wait for World War III to start.

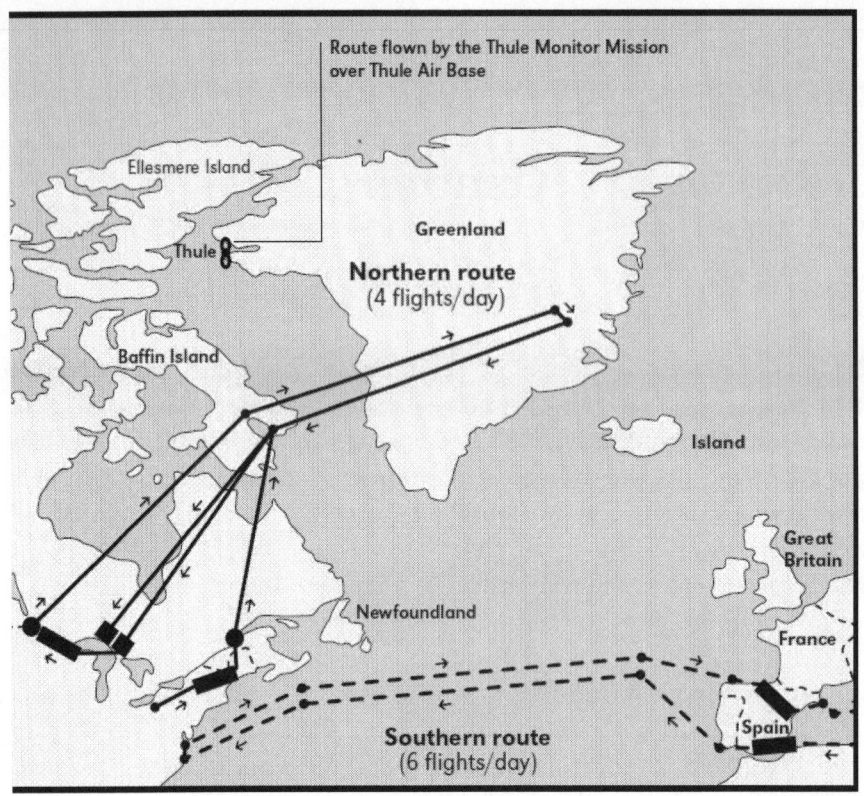

Chrome Dome Routes, Showing Southern Route from East Coast
Image courtesy of the USAF

This was SAC, the Strategic Air Command. It is pronounced *sack*, never S-A-C. General Curtis LeMay built it into a powerful machine, and it was designed to be the elite fighting force for a new battle concept, total annihilation of the Soviet Union. The necessity for the Strategic Air Command had its beginnings in the Northern Mariana Islands in 1944. That's when General LeMay unleashed the fury of massive bombing on the mainland of Japan from Guam, Saipan, and Tinian. Hundreds of long-range B-29's hammered the enemy with a pace never before seen in history. The only pause was whenever LeMay ran out of bombs, and had to wait while the Navy resupplied his airfields from their supply ships. On the night of March 9-10, 1945, incendiary bombs started a raging firestorm and destroyed sixteen square miles of Tokyo and killed almost one hundred thousand people. LeMay would later say that he might be tried as a war criminal if Japan had won the war. The Joint Chiefs of Staff in Washington found his military successes hard to comprehend. How could a bomber command, on a tiny island in the Pacific, thousands of miles from America's shores, singlehandedly be so effective against such a powerhouse as Japan?

It was two single B-29s, with two single bombs, that brought Japan to its knees without an invasion, but it was the overwhelming air power that laid the groundwork. General James H. "Jimmy" Doolittle said, "The Navy had the transport to make the invasion of Japan possible; the Ground Forces had the power to make it successful; and the B-29 made it unnecessary."

General Hap Arnold said, "The influence of atomic energy on air power can be stated very simply. It has made air power all-important."

There, in the Pacific, with the B-29 and the atomic bomb, air power entered its primacy. It showed what massive air power and the atomic bomb could do. The seeds for the Strategic Air Command were sown.

LeMay had the nickname Old Iron Ass. When he took over a B-24 bomber group in Europe, the mission abort rate was high. He told the crews that he would fly the lead on every mission, and any crew who aborted would be court-martialed. He was not the first commander of the Strategic Air Command, but he is considered its father. When he took over as SAC commander in 1948, it had just a few untrained B-29 groups that were World War II leftovers, and only half of them were operational. The officer force was demoralized and training was far from adequate. As an early exercise, he had his planners set up a simulated bombing attack. The target: Wright Field, now known as Wright-Patterson Air Force Base, Dayton, Ohio. It was to be a practice radar bomb run, at night, from thirty thousand feet using the entire SAC fleet of five hundred bombers. It was a disaster. Not a single plane accomplished its mission. Only 303 planes reached the target, none hit it, and the average miss was 10,090 feet, almost two miles. LeMay had his work cut out for him. By July 1950, the circular error amount was down to 2,600 feet, then down to 1,925 feet, acceptable for nuclear war.

LeMay had promised that he would defeat Japan from the air in World War II, and he kept that promise. He promised he would keep Berlin open from the air at the start of the Cold War, and he did it. He promised that SAC could deliver annihilation from the air against our enemies under any condition, at any time, and he was keeping that promise too. He had stated, "The objective of our national defense police is deterrence. In the public mind—both ours and the Soviets—deterrence is rooted in fear of nuclear devastation of population centers." LeMay would be a general for seventeen years, longer than any other man in the history of the United States military. He was the youngest four-star general since Ulysses S. Grant. He would be awarded every medal but one, the Medal of Honor. His ever-present cigar was partly to hide a drooping lip from Bell's palsy, which was caused by flying high and cold.

Two months after LeMay took over SAC, Air Force Chief of Staff General Hoyt Vandenberg called a meeting. It was held at Maxwell Air Force Base in Montgomery, Alabama. It was on December 6, 1948, seven years to the day after the attack on Pearl Harbor. All the Air Force commanders were there to discuss force readiness in a darkened conference room, complete with impressive slide discussions. General John Montgomery, the SAC planner, in somber and unflinching tones spelled out the tactics and timelines for destroying the Soviet Union's cities and defenses. One attendee remembered, "It was the voice of doom."

LeMay was present in the conference room, but his part of the show-and-tell was not yet ready, it was still en route to Maxwell. Without telling his boss, LeMay had scheduled a performance that would nail down the roll of air power. He had two bombers, launched from Carswell Air Force Base in Texas, not stripped down, but in war configuration, to haul a load of dummy bombs to a spot just off the shores of Hawaii to the approximate longitude of Pearl Harbor, and drop them in the sea at about the same time of day the Japanese attacked seven years before. It was a round trip of 7,700 miles, and several refuelings were necessary. There is now some discussion as to what type planes were involved, but according to Doug Keeney, it was one B-36 and a B-50, modified for midair refueling. They were supposed to land back at Maxwell, right at the site of the conference, but they had to divert at the last minute due to a base-scheduling problem. The point was well-made however. SAC could deliver an atomic bomb anywhere in the world.

Many people in the 1950s and 1960s believed with almost religious fervor that it was SAC alone that kept them safe from the Soviets. Most believed we were always on the brink of nuclear war. This was the time of underground fallout shelters, *duck and cover*, and schoolchildren wearing their dog tags, so their bodies could be identified after the coming nuclear holocaust. When the television networks went off the air at 1:00 a.m., they played the National Anthem, and it was frequently a flight of B-52s that flew across an image of the flag.

In 1960, the Western Union Telegraph Company patented the Nuclear Bomb Explosion Detection Device. It was designed to look like a telephone pole transformer, but with a sensor that would detect only explosions from nuclear bombs, as opposed to lightning. It was placed around eighty-four military targets and thirteen cities, and would notify

SAC, the Pentagon, and the North American Air Defense Command Headquarters if the signature of a nuclear thermal flash was detected.

LeMay's thinking, based on his World War II experience, what that massive, overwhelming force was the only way to fight a war. He had done it in Japan, and the new United States Air Force would soon get 46 percent of America's defense budget. SAC doubled its personnel in five years, from 1950 to 1955. The new president, Dwight Eisenhower, joined LeMay's "church of deterrence," and America could prevent nuclear war only by showing spectacular strength. Handling the workload of this responsibility was on the bombers alone, the B-36, the B-47, and the B-52. ICBMs were just not in the picture yet. Even though the Atlas missile was declared operational in 1959 by General Power, a year later, he would say, "Missile reliability . . . still causes me deep concern. As a result of our experience at Vandenberg with Atlas, our probability of a successful launch . . . is almost zero."

The learning curve of getting such a large organization as SAC up and running definitely was difficult. Here are three examples of accidents that LeMay dealt with in the 1950s:

July 27, 1956. A B-47 with no weapons aboard had completed a training mission and was conducting touch-and-go landings at Lakenheath RAF Station, England, about twenty miles from Cambridge. The aircraft had just made its fourth landing when it veered off the runway and into a storage igloo. Inside the igloo were three Mark 6 fission weapons. No nuclear capsules were involved but each weapon had approximately five thousand pounds of high explosive. The bombs did not detonate or burn and there was no radiation contamination. The four airmen aboard the B-47 were killed. "Without a nuclear capsule the Mark 6 contained only natural uranium and a one-point detonation would not have turned the eastern part of England into a desert as has been stated by other sources." (Maggelet and Oskins, *Broken Arrow, Vol I*).

October 11, 1957. At Homestead AFB, Florida, a B-47, with a Mark 6 nuclear weapon aboard, was number one for takeoff when the tower called and advised that an outrigger tire appeared to be blown. The aircraft was told to hold and maintenance would check the tire. A few seconds later the aircraft started the takeoff roll and transmitted that they would see how it felt while rolling. At the six-thousand-foot mark on the runway the tower advised the aircraft that the outrigger landing gear was on fire. The aircraft reduced power then reapplied power in an attempt to get off the ground, taking off with nose high, right wing low. It crashed and burned for four hours. All four crewmen died. The weapon and a nuclear capsule and its carrying case were recovered intact.

November 4, 1958. Dyess Air Force Base, Abilene, Texas. A B-47 with either a Mark 15 or Mark 39 was standing ready for an alert test requiring takeoff. At 9:20 a.m. the Klaxon sounded, and the aircraft taxied out and began the takeoff roll using the jet assisted take-off bottles, which are a group of rockets temporarily affixed to the aircraft, to assist in proving take-off power. When they are ignited they burn until the solid fuel in them is exhausted. There is no way to turn them off. After take off, when the aircraft is airborne, they are used up and they are jettisoned. Something went wrong—at least one of the bottles malfunctioned and kicked sideways, its flames hitting the fuselage. The aircraft caught fire on takeoff, shedding multiple pieces of aircraft and burning furiously. The aircraft commander made a conscious effort to get the airplane to five hundred feet altitude so the downward ejecting navigator could get out. Then he turned thirty degrees in an effort to avoid populated areas. The three crewmen with ejection seats safely bailed out but the crew chief without an ejection seat died in the crash. The resulting detonation from high explosive created a crater thirty-five feet wide and six feet deep.

Several years before the flight of *Keep 19*, SAC had begun developing a new game plan, to press as the aggressor against the opponent. One of the first goals was to gain control of the nation's nuclear weapons for the bombers. The weapons had always been under the control of the Atomic Energy Commission, a civilian agency. LeMay wanted a faster way to get his hands on the weapons, to get *bombs-on-base*, so they would be available immediately on Strategic Air Command bases, and not have to wait for them to be checked out of the stockpile storage facilities. He not only wanted them available on base, he wanted them on the bombers. In order to do that, he had to prove that SAC's people were trained and qualified, and that the proper equipment and procedures were in place. That was exactly what SAC was good at: training, qualifications, and procedures. Once those factors were in place, LeMay could add the next feature, speed.

Sometimes however, speed worked against him. Speed and the art of bomb loading, for example, did not go well together. Take what happened on the morning of March 11, 1958, at Hunter Air Force Base outside of Savannah, Georgia. A bomb-loading crew was hurrying through the process of loading a thirty-kiloton MK-6 nuclear weapon onto a B-47, scheduled for a flight to England. The B-47s did not have a way to dump fuel, so the crews needed a fast way of safely jettisoning the heavy, unarmed bomb in the event of power loss on takeoff. The copilot, who sat in tandem right behind the pilot, did this job. He would remotely remove a steel safety pin from the bomb's release mechanism for takeoff, in order to allow an emergency jettison if needed. He would then replace the pin when safely airborne.

That morning, the bomb-loading team had a tight safety pin, and they encouraged its seating by use of a big hammer. They did not have time to go through the engage/disengage cycle of removing the pin. They were running out of time, and if they missed the stated finish bomb-load time, they would lose points. Someone decided to skip the engage/disengage cycle check.

Before takeoff, copilot Captain Charles Woodruff removed the pin as required and they had an on-time takeoff. At five thousand feet, Captain Woodruff attempted to engage the pin, but it would not insert. They could not continue the mission with the pin out. He tried many times but it just would not engage. Captain Earl Koehler, the pilot, instructed the navigator/bombardier, Captain Bruce Kulka, to go back to the bomb bay and try to "fix the problem." Captain Kulka, removed his parachute in order to fit through the opening in the bomb bay. He crawled in the bomb bay, but since he was a small man, could not see over the roundness of the huge bomb, five feet wide and ten feet long, filling the bomb bay. He jumped up, spreading his body over the bomb, feeling around in the tight space above the bomb. What he grabbed was the bomb release cable.

The bomb, with Captain Kulka spread out on top, released and fell a few inches against the bomb bay doors. Stunned, Kulka grabbed hold of something. The doors flipped open under the weight of the 7,600-pound bomb and it fell toward Mars Bluff, South Carolina, with Captain Kulka hanging on to the aircraft as if his life depended on it. It did.

The crew circled and watched a shock wave radiate out from the concussion when the high explosives in the bomb went off. It did not have the *pit* installed, so there was no danger of nuclear detonation. It did have several hundred pounds of high explosive.

They could not raise Hunter Air Force Base on the radio, so they had to ask—broadcasting in the clear—that nearby Florence Municipal Airport call the Air Force base at Savannah and tell them they had just dropped a nuclear weapon accidentally. No, they did not know the telephone number. Florence had to call collect. While they circled to burn off fuel and to watch the three-thousand-foot plume of smoke, the only thing Captain Kulka would say was, "We would be better off going to Brazil."

He became known in the Air Force as the Nuclear Navigator. After Vietnam, he moved to Thailand and never answered his mail.

No one on the ground was killed, but three were injured. Walter Gregg, the farmer who was bombed, settled with the Air Force for $54,000, for the total destruction of the house, contents, trucks, and "six to fourteen" chickens. The Air Force couldn't determine the exact number of chickens because they were vaporized.

The bomb crater is still there, on Crater Road, at Mars Bluff, South Carolina, east of Florence. Chunks of the bomb are on display in the Florence Museum.

As part of SAC's new push for power, a subtle change in the wording of the *Emergency War Plan* was made in the late 1950s. The title was changed to the *Emergency War Order*, implying they were through with planning—they were now ready for orders.

Another view of the SAC philosophy was revealed years later in an interview with former Soviet officials. It concerned land-based ICBM missile silos that were not *hardened* by constructing them as underground facilities; instead, they were grouped tightly together, and considered *soft* targets, easily taken out by the Soviets. They knew the Americans "were not stupid" they knew the silos were easily visible to Soviet satellite photography. The Soviets then realized these ICBMs were not designed to ride out a strike. Instead, they were meant to be used as first strike weapons. Not only that, but SAC wanted the Soviets to know it.

General LeMay demanded hard work, pride, but most of all, professionalism from the crews. He insisted on rigorous training and extremely high standards of performance for his aircrews. SAC's official historian once explained, "If you weren't in SAC you simply did not have the high sense of urgency. You could not keep up." The annual written proficiency tests required a score of 100 percent to pass. A 99 percent score failed. Alert crews were constantly being tested on their specialties. Any score below 100 percent required more lectures, more study, and another test. The testing during alert duty became so frequent that crews begged to be tested before lectures. If they passed, they could skip that day's lecture.

LeMay was a ham radio hobbyist, and he incorporated his knowledge of single-sideband radio into practice. He knew that, combined with midair refueling, constant radio communication with his bombers was absolutely essential for a worldwide airborne alert system. Single-sideband modulation (SSB) was the only convenient system at that time to have thousands of miles of range. LeMay had an SSB transceiver put on a bomber and told his deputy, Lieutenant General Francis Griswald, also an amateur radio operator, to "go fly around some." Griswald flew to the Far East, while chatting with LeMay in Okinawa. A larger test involving a dozen ham radio stations on the ground and in airplanes, proved the viability of constant radio communications with SAC bombers.

In the years to come, communications systems would become increasingly complex and reliable. Knowing that any intelligence monitoring by the Soviets would measure the amount of military radio chatter as a degree of force activity, the Air Force added white noise (meaningless messages and raw data) into the mix of true communications to fill the gaps, just to increase chatter. The right equipment on the other end filtered out this noise. Other systems were added to cover the possibility of headquarters being wiped out in a strike:

- The airborne command post known as Looking Glass, constantly manned with a General officer aboard,
- A network of rockets to be launched that would carry transmitters for Go Codes,
- A low frequency radio system using the Earth itself as the transmitter; so-called *Earth waves*. This last system unofficially was named Thumper, for the slow, measured *thump* of each letter received at wing command posts and missile silos.

Voice messages received at Command Posts on the older radios would sound something like this: "Break-break. This is a High Hat message in seventeen parts. Authentication Code Zulu, Four, Hotel, Zulu. Part one: India, Bravo, Tango, November, Juliet. Part two . . . " At command posts all over the SAC net, people would write down columns of five letters, which would be converted into columns of five numbers, which would be converted into English words. The five-digit code was old school, as old as the Civil War, but it was still used in the 1960s alongside the newer encrypted messages systems.

LeMay was a tough commander, but he wanted to create special benefits of being a member of SAC, one of which was the temporary promotion policy. Commanders had the authority to recommend selected individuals and crews to be temporarily promoted one step up in both rank and pay grade, based on performance. This was certainly an incentive. When SAC first started it sometimes operated out of tar-paper shacks on overseas bases, now LeMay was having modern buildings constructed and decent housing built. The alert facilities had swimming pools and picnic areas for family visits. Some of the alert-facility cooks trained in fine hotels to learn how to create culinary masterpieces. SAC had a million-dollar telephone and Teletype network to link all bases to Omaha headquarters. Crewmembers wore white ascots with their flight suits. LeMay had turned SAC into an elite outfit. And they were the big dogs with the nuclear hammer.

Each crew on alert could get a dark blue Air Force station wagon or four-door pickup truck whenever they needed to be away from the alert facility, as long as they stayed on base and within the sound of the Klaxon. They had to be able to get back to their aircraft and meet the required take-off time, so everywhere they went on base, there were special parking spots marked with yellow paint, and a sign that read, ALERT CREW PARKING ONLY. Such spots were at any place they may need to go: the base exchange, the commissary, the credit union, Officer's Club, library, movie theater, even the base chapel. If it was a place with seats like the chapel or theater the last two rows of seats closest to the exit always were reserved for alert crews, marked in yellow. Their families could meet them there, but would know to quickly step aside when the horn went off, or if the movie stopped and the words ALERT CREWS RESPOND appeared on the movie screen. If one of the crew needed to do something on base away from the alert facility, like cash a check at the credit union, several of them would sign out a vehicle, drive over to the credit union, and proceed to the head of the line to take care of business. Whenever an alert crewmember broke a line, if anyone behind them had a problem with that they would certainly keep it to themselves.

The author witnessed, during the 1962 Cuban Missile Crisis, the right to break line at the commissary, the base food store. It was a somber occasion. The wives of alert crewmen were waiting, each with several food shopping carts filled with cases of canned goods, lined up along the wall of the commissary. When the blue alert vehicles pulled up to the curb, each crewman went to his family, and had a very serious, very emotional talk with them. Then they went to the head of the line and checked out.

Outside, they loaded the food into family vehicles, mostly campers and trucks. There was another serious, emotional talk with the kids and wives, and tearful good-byes all around.

Then, the families drove off to someplace safe. The crewmembers watched them go, then got in their bright blue trucks and drove back to the alert facility, to be near their loaded aircraft.

Every New Year's Day the annual Commanders' Reception was held at the Officer's Club on SAC bases. Officers' wives would dress in long formal wear, the male officers not on alert would wear the infamous *mess dress* uniform, which had a short tuxedo jacket that looked like it belonged to a waiter. That was for the male officers. Female officers' mess dress uniforms looked like they belonged to another waiter.

All would meet at the O Club at noon, for cocktails, hors d'oeuvres, and social small talk. The officers would leave their card, an actual calling card, in a silver dish. This is the only time the card was used in the history of the US Air Force as far as anyone knows. Those on alert stood out just a wee bit. They couldn't drink, and they always tended to stick together. They would meet their wives at the front door of the club, and escort them through the reception line. Their wives would be in classic formal wear, the husbands would dress in stylish, rumpled, green flight suits, sometimes with pistols in shoulder holsters.

Combat and support crews went through enough stress just to be in SAC: long periods of time away from families, the stress of the constant care of the weapons, working long hours on the flight line, often in terrible weather. It seemed like many SAC bases were located where there was extreme weather. In fact, a lot were, to be close to the Soviet Union via Arctic routes. But the East Coast route went to the milder climes of Spain and the Mediterranean. A guessing game of crews concerned the source of the name Chrome Dome. The B-52s at that time were painted the *nuclear blast reflection* pattern: light gray on top, brilliant white on the bottom. And supposedly there would be so many of them flying overhead that from below it would look like an aluminum overcast, hence the name chrome dome.

The temporary spot promotion policy for some SAC Select crews was certainly an incentive, but it sometimes had its drawbacks. If anyone on a crew screwed up badly, and it reflected on the crew's performance, that entire crew could lose their temporary spot promotions and get knocked back to their permanent grades with the lower pay. This certainly adversely affected the morale of that crew, but that was nothing compared to the morale of the wives. If somebody on the crew caused a drop in the grocery money, there would definitely be problems on the home front, directed at whatever crewmember was *the goat*.

On Sunday evening, January 22, 1961, the members of crew R-10 were released from the alert facility to go to their quarters for rest. They had completed the four days of alert duty and were now ready to fly a real mission. The next morning, at 8:00 a.m., they reported for duty and had the traditional hot breakfast in the alert facility mess hall. After breakfast, they gathered for the pre-takeoff briefing at 8:45 a.m. All six regular crewmembers of R-10 were present, plus the extras, third pilot First Lieutenant Mattocks, and Major Richards. During the weather portion of the briefing, the gunner, Sergeant Barnish went to the base in-flight kitchen as usual to pick up the preordered flight meals and put them on their tabs. Officers paid $1.35, enlisted paid 95¢.

Only Known Photo of Lieutenant Adam Mattocks in the Air Force. Here he is a very young student pilot. The photo is probably from the 1950s.
Image courtesy of the Mattocks family

*Major Eugene Richards.
Image courtesy USAF.*

They boarded their waiting aircraft and then became call sign *Keep 19*, the radio name for this mission, and had an on-time takeoff at 10:56 a.m. on Monday, January 23, 1961.

They would crash about thirteen hours later, shortly after midnight on January 24, 1961. Five of the crew would survive; three would die.

The Last Three Hours And Six Minutes of *Keep 19*

Keep 19 completed the first scheduled midair refueling without incident, but now turbulence was picking up along the assigned corridor. The cold front was behind them and moving them along to the east, both tanker and bomber, like surfers riding a ground swell. The winds aloft would later be estimated as out of the west at over 150 knots at 40,000 feet. *Keep 19* was assigned 29,000 feet.

Midair refueling was absolutely essential for SAC's mission of worldwide bomber coverage. It had its awkward beginning with a British concept called the *looped hose* method in which a tanker, trailing a hose behind it, flew in front of the receiver aircraft. The receiver would fly a dangling grapple hook over a loop and haul the hose aboard. It was installed on the B-29, and proficiency training began. The Air Force finally had its global reach. A new day had dawned.

Two methods of midair refueling were soon developed: the *probe-and-drogue* and the flying boom, a forty-foot telescoping boom from the bottom of a tanker that could be maneuvered into the refueling receptacle of the bomber. The Navy and Marines still use the probe-and-drogue, but SAC wanted the flying boom, and wanted the receptacle of the receiving airplane placed outside the pilot's field of vision whenever possible. Refueling formation flying was difficult enough. SAC did not want the pilot to watch the nozzle as it approached, leave that to the boom operator. On the B-52, the opening is in the top of the fuselage, back behind the pilots and forward of the EW and gunner.

By the early 60s, there was one SAC refueling every 6.8 minutes somewhere in the world. Twelve B-52s were authorized for the first three Chrome Dome routes in early 1961. To refuel these twelve bombers, tankers were expected to pump a minimum of 634,000 gallons a day, or over 50,000 gallons per day per bomber. Tanker aircraft and crews stood alert just like the bomber crews: airplanes ready and cocked, pointed at forty-five degrees to the runway on their herringbone, or *Christmas Tree* parking ramps. Just like the bombers, the tankers were ready—fueled up, departure frequencies pre-set on the radios, navigation charts, checklists, and sunglasses on the seats. Headsets were plugged in. The aircraft was ready for the crews to dash to the plane, pausing long enough to give the correct number code to the armed security guard. SAC Combat Defense guards didn't assume that just because you had a flight suit and a flight line badge you were legit; you didn't get past without knowing the daily code. One pilot remembered: "If we were running out to the aircraft we wouldn't cross the red line until we knew the number. If the number was five the guard would hold up two fingers and we'd hold up three and he would let us through. If you crossed the red line without the guard approving, you might just get shot." At the very least, you would definitely be standing in front of a desk later, getting yelled at by someone with a lot of insignia on his collar.

The KC-135 jet tanker was a big improvement over the older prop-driven KC-97, which struggled to match the much faster B-47 Stratojet in the 1950s. The pilots of the two-plane formation worked out a ticklish maneuver to compensate this difference in speed. The KC-97—going balls to the wall—the throttles shoved full forward toward the instrument panel wall at the maximum speed; while the streamlined B-47 slowed to near stall speed. Then the hook-up at high altitude was followed by a shallow dive, in tandem. Both could speed up, making for better control of both aircraft while the refueling took place.

On that Monday at various times Lieutenant Mattocks had replaced Major Tulloch and Captain Rardin for rest and relief. They were now setting up for the second refueling scheduled for 29,000 feet near Columbia, South Carolina, at around 9:00 p.m. Their tanker was designated *Addle 57*. The boomer (often called Casey, because he lowers the refueling boom) was in his pod, looking down on them from above, waiting. Boomers were enlisted men, and would brag they had a great job: ride in the back lying down while two officers drove them around.

The B-52 was bigger than the KC-135 tanker, and flying while it took on a large, shifting weight of fuel was a handful. Wrestling with the BUFF, estimating the reaction time of the spoiler delay during the refueling, was exhausting, especially during turbulence.

According to the government document *The History Of Flight*, this is what happened next:

> Rendezvous was six minutes early. The initial [*refueling*] contact was held only for a few seconds with an outer limit disconnect being experienced. The second contact was made and held until 93,000 pounds of fuel had been onloaded. At this time the receiver pilot [*Major Tulloch*] disconnected and returned to the observation position to rest a few minutes. *[Lieutenant Mattocks took over left seat]*. It should be noted that the tanker was being hand flown by the tanker copilot for a short time during the refueling. After the receiver pilot rested a few minutes, the tanker was requested to increase airspeed to 260 KIAS *[knots indicated air speed]* and another contact was established. After three disconnects had occurred, the Boom Operator reported a fuel leak coming from the right wing behind the number three nacelle. (Italics added.)

Major Tulloch was working hard. After the first disengagement and the partial load, he backed away and asked Mattocks to fly while he stretched out on the pad on the floor. Speeding up helped. Then three more quick disconnects. Between the slow spoiler response and air turbulence from the boundary front, it must have been frustrating. The pressure was on to complete this heavyweight refueling mission and get qualified for Chrome Dome. Lieutenant Mattocks was back in his IP seat behind the two pilots and looking over their shoulders at the instrument panels. He said he saw the drop on Number 4 fuel tank. Major Tulloch reset the gauge to test it. It dropped to zero like it was supposed to, then slowly began to climb, but it never showed full.

The B-52 crew could not see the fuel leak from the cockpit since the wing was behind them. Major Tulloch had Captain Rardin ask the tanker to drop back and under to take a look, but the crew of *Addle 57* couldn't see very well in the dark. Major Tulloch asked Seymour Johnson to get a chase plane ready to come up at dawn and get a good look. The three pilots worked the checklist for refueling leaks.

Major Tulloch at first did not think they were in immediate danger, but agreed with the Command Post to return to the Seymour Johnson area. *Addle 57* moved out one mile ahead and one thousand feet above them, well out of range of an explosion. The boom operator was watching closely. Tulloch made sure that the tower was keeping the Command Post informed of the fuel problems.

It was later determined that the initial fuel loss amounted to thirty-seven thousand pounds, or about nineteen tons in a little over two minutes. That would be at the rate of thirty-six gallons per second. This is almost comparable to the water drop ability of the huge Martin Mars airborne forest firefighter, now used in Canada. Over the entire three-hour period of the emergency, total fuel loss would be fifty-four tons. They had been flying for ten hours and thirty-three minutes at that time.

Once again, the tanker was asked to take another look from behind, but this time above *Keep 19*. This time, *Addle 57* got a better angle and reported the leak between engine pod number three and the fuselage. The decision was made to leave the area and go out to sea beyond Wilmington, North Carolina, about thirty minutes away. By deciding to get out over the water, the level of the emergency just went up one level with the crew. An attempted emergency fuel purge of tank number three was unsuccessful due to pump problems. They would have to get rid of the fuel in that tank by using it up in the engines.

The wing commander had been called at his quarters at Seymour Johnson, and he was now in his staff car on the way to the Command Post. He used his car radio to talk directly with Major Tulloch. Headquarters SAC was notified of the in-flight emergency. The full expertise of the Air Force was up and running. Boeing Airplane Company was notified, including nearby military bases and even the Wilmington and Oak Island Coast Guard Stations. Major Tulloch wanted to hear from the chief of the standardization crew, similar to an airline's chief pilot. He was a trusted and knowledgeable friend.

Major Tulloch said, "It would probably be a good idea to shut down the two engines." Normally fuel venting at that altitude was not combustible, but that amount of fuel pouring into the exhaust of jet engines is another matter. He shut down the two closest engines on the right wing, number's five and six, to reduce the risk of fire. However, shutting down those engines stopped the hydraulics and generator systems for the right side, disabling controls for the right wing. Lieutenant Mattocks quickly opened circuits from the left side generator to run the right side controls.

By this time, they were out over the Atlantic Ocean and Keep 19 was instructed to orbit at thirty thousand feet with the in-bound turning point no closer than ten miles east of Wilmington. The object was to keep the aircraft well away from populated areas, but close enough for Coast Guard rescue if necessary. They now had to use excessive trim to maintain control.

Major Tulloch needed someone to check out the bomb bay. The only crew access to the bomb bay in flight was through the forward wheel well via the small door that was Major Richards' backrest. That would mean breaching the pressure bulkhead. Any trip to the bomb bay in flight would require going down into the Hole, passing through the forward wheel well and squeezing around the stowed landing gear, a tight fit. Sergeant Frank Barnish, the smallest man on the airplane, was just the guy.

This meant leaving his parachute on his ejection seat because there wasn't going to be enough room to wear it where he was going. He first switched his oxygen mask connection over to the walk-around oxygen bottle, for that was required when they were depressurized above twelve thousand five hundred feet, and they were at thirty thousand feet. Frank climbed down the ladder into the navigators' Hole. Major Richards probably wanted to know what was going on up on the flight deck. The two may have been talking with each other helmet-to-helmet instead of using the crew-wide interphone. The major had moved out of his spot at the back of the Hole while Frank waited for the airplane to be depressurized. Then Frank looked through the round porthole widow in the door, just to be sure nothing bad was waiting for him, like fire or an open wheel well, then he unlatched the bulkhead pressure door. This depressurizing process is similar to what happens at the end of each flight when the engines spool down and the ground crew puts the wheel chocks in place. Before cracking open the crew door hatch in the bottom of the airplane, the navigator calls the pilot on the interphone: "Navigator to pilot: Is your window open?" Unlatching the crew hatch without first completely depressurizing the airplane could cause the crew hatch door to blast downward with disastrous results—either an injured ground crew, or a damaged hatch with sprung hinges, or both. Opening the pilot's side window insures equal air pressure throughout the airplane. If the hatch blew open, the bomber could be taken out of the alert rotation while the door was repaired or replaced, just because the pilot's window was not opened the specified four inches. Of course, opening a window in flight was not an option, so the copilot controlled the cabin pressure valves, which depressurized the plane.

Keeping a B-52 pressurized in flight is an essential function, and it is powered by a very complicated system. A former BUFF crewman, Lothar "Nick" Maier, facetiously explained it this way: The B-52 is a masterpiece of engineering, but a big part of its nervous system is determined by the quality of duct tape mending of the single greatest concept of aircraft design: the *air bleed system*. This is a complex monstrosity of four-inch wide piping and manifolds carrying air at about 750°F and 250 pounds per square inch pressure. The air pressure starts at the final compressor stage of each of the eight jet engines. This superheated, pressurized air circulates throughout the entire airframe in a twisting, pulsating, screaming manifold of threatening, potentially dangerous hot air leaks. An *internal inferno* designed to deliver essential operating pressure to wherever required, such as the horizontal stabilizer movement and the crew compartment pressurization and air conditioning and heating. It is also the power source for secondary engine start—all from the windmills in the engines.

This hostile environment awaited Frank Barnish as he entered the forward wheel well. The noise must have been unbelievable—the whistling of the outside airstream, the screaming of the air bleed system manifolds, the stink of the JP-4 jet fuel that had poured down from the massive leak above. He struggled aft through his inspection tour, crawling around and over the big rubber wheels, along the shuttering crawlspace, constantly on the lookout for dangerous air bleed leaks, on into the bomb bays. He returned to the flight deck stinking of the fuel on his flight suit. He must have had very bad flashbacks of bailing out over Germany. That didn't go so well back then, in World War II.

When Frank returned, he reported to Major Tulloch that the bomb bay was covered in jet fuel. The entire wheel well was soaked, and it was covering not only the bottom of the hull but much of the electronic equipment. Frank went back to his ejection seat and refastened his parachute and changed his oxygen supply back to the connection on the seat. One spark could turn the aircraft into a massive fireball, and he wanted very badly to be ready to punch out, quickly eject—through the fireball if necessary—but just get out of the airplane.

The crew began pulling circuit breakers, including most interior lights. They flew on, in a wide loop shaped like a racetrack, trying to minimize the chance of fire and to stabilize the giant aircraft. The refueling tanker, *Addle 57*, stayed on the scene. Now another problem: the EW had been having trouble with the HF radio, and the ARAC 58 radio was inoperative.

As they made gentle turns out over the dark Atlantic, the pilots had to increase the trim controls to help maintain attitude and altitude of the bomber to compensate for the changing weight. During this time the Command Post was relaying instructions to Keep 19 in regards to fuel management. The fuel transfer pumps were acting erratically or not at all at times. It created a series of continuous adjustments for Rardin and Mattocks. They would pump fuel and switch tanks, trying to balance the airplane by using the consumption of the engines alone where possible.

Everyone on board was aware of the growth of things going wrong—the fuel leak, the pump failures, and now radio failures. Could they all be connected? Is this how accident reports are written up?

Pilots and crew are a suspicious bunch. They are always on the lookout for unusual events, noises, smells, and vibrations—anything unusual gives them pause. They are also extremely aware of time and its passage. It is said the three most useless things to a pilot are altitude above you, runway behind you, and two seconds ago.

The crew tried everything they knew to resolve the crisis. After more than two hours, Washington Center cleared them to depart the Wilmington area, and head north to their home base, Seymour Johnson. Major Tulloch told Captain Rardin, "Tell them I said I intend to stay in the Wilmington area to use up more fuel." This led to a discussion with the wing commander, who wanted him back at the base, so Major Tulloch lost in that discussion. After one more orbit at sea, "radar revealed the coast line." Major Tulloch would say in his narrative that he agreed with the decision to land. He had always said it was his responsibility and all decisions were up to him as aircraft commander.

He had recently read a report of another bomber that had made it down safely under similar circumstances, but the plane had burst into flames on the runway after it landed. He warned his crew to be ready to make tracks as soon as they could land and stop. Keep 19 now crossed the North Carolina coast near Wrightsville Beach. The crew had some time to think and knew they were in trouble, but the aircraft at least at this point appeared to be balanced and was handling well.

Paul Brown's clock on the navigator's panel reached midnight. Twenty-four hundred hours. Monday was over and Tuesday was starting. The crew thought the airplane was under control, fuel management appeared to be working, and airspeed was not an issue even with the two right side engines out. They loosened the tight, uncomfortable chin straps of their helmets and tried to relax. In the clear moonlit night above the Carolina countryside and towns, *Keep 19* was heading north toward home, early.

But on the right wing, above and behind the crew, a metal fatigue crack was growing inside the second panel of wing section number 556. The crack could not have been found by the ground maintenance people on preflight inspection. The inspection had been done exactly as specified. Sure, there was a general statement about looking for wrinkles and cracks in all exterior wing, control, and fuselage skin, just as it has always been for every airplane, from the Piper Cub to the Boeing 707, and all crew chiefs knew all about metal fatigue cracks and how to fix them: drill 'em and stick 'em—drill a clean, exact hole and fill it with the right size rivet. They always found stress wrinkles, but it was the seriousness of any problem that was the tough call. If every aircraft was grounded for every skin defect found, few would fly, especially in the B-52 fleet. In fact, the hidden weakness in this wing design was already known at higher levels. But raising the issue of a wing problem would mean taking any B-52 out of service, and Chrome Dome and the Airborne Alert were just starting. Anyway, this airplane was scheduled to go out of service and to the repair depot in four months, on May 5, 1961.

Right then, in the first minutes of that Tuesday, their immediate concern was to finish this ride and prove that the crew was proficient enough to haul two MK-39 thermonuclear devices around, ready to drop, for a period of twenty-five hours, the length of time it takes to fly to the Mediterranean and loiter on station. That would put them as Qualified, Chrome Dome, Southern Route.

The crack in the wing panel was growing.

Also growing, like an aortic aneurysm, was a weakness in at least one of the fuel lines couplets. This was part of the system that connected together the big fuel compartments that made up the interior of the wing, known as a *wet wing*. When the wings moved in flight, and they did a lot of moving, the flexible lines and couplets had to take up any slack, and move in any direction. The first type of couplets used were known as Marman clamps, and they broke down from the start of G- and F-model operations. They caused *fuel gushers,* whose name alone would indicate a very serious flying hazard. Several repair projects were tried such as the CF-14 Blue Band, and the CF-17 Hard Shell, but were obviously not foolproof solutions. We are not sure which clamp was used on this aircraft. Herbert Marx, better known as Zeppo (one of the Marx Brothers) invented Marman clamps.

Each crewmember mentally went through the bail out drill, just in case. The four crewmen on the top level would eject upward, and the two on the lower level would eject downward. It was specified that as soon as the navigator on the lower level had ejected, the two extras, the men not in ejection seats, would make their way to the lower deck hatch opening and drop through it, then manually deploy their parachutes. That was the general concept, and there was a recommended bail out sequence to follow if the bail out was elective and they had enough time. Since the crew is confined to a relatively small portion of the aircraft, in a controlled bail out it would be better if they did not go out all at once, but one at a time to prevent the possibility of high speed midair collisions with each other. The navigator, Paul Brown, would go first. Reason: they needed that opening in the bottom of the airplane for the two extras to jump through—Richards and Mattocks. There was no other way for those two guys without ejection seats to get out of the airplane. That's why it was the navigator to go first: he happened to be sitting directly over the ejection hatch cover which was the closest to the ladder between decks, and that was the best egress point for the extras. Gene Shelton was to stay in his ejection seat for a short time, right beside that opening, to render assistance to anyone that needed it. He was the guy who made sure that anybody who was supposed to go through that opening in the floor did so.

Next in the controlled bail out sequence would be the two non-pilots on the upper deck: Sergeant Barnish, the gunner, and Captain Wilson, the EW. They would eject upward. Then Major Shelton would eject downward. Next, the copilot Captain Rardin would go. Last would be the commander of the ship, Major Tulloch, after assuring that all others had left the aircraft. All this was making the assumption that the crew had sufficient time, and the bomber would be under reasonable control and flying horizontal. Bomber ejection seats were catapults, powered by explosive-powered compressed air cylinders rather than the rockets found in the single-seater fighters. Bomber crews sat side-by-side, and the flaming exhaust of a rocket taking off right next to someone is not a good idea for the second guy—much better to have a compressed air catapult.

PLANNED BAILOUT ROUTES

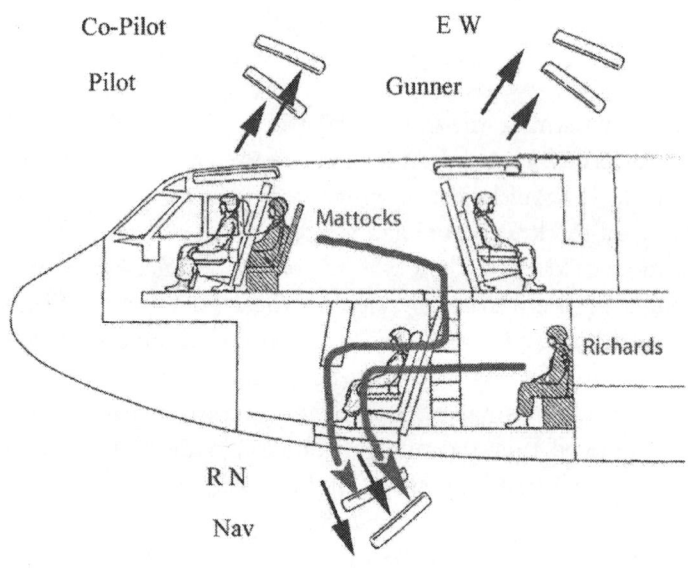

Planned Bail Out Routes.
Image courtesy USAF, modified by author.

There was also another very good reason for the order of a controlled bail out, it had to do with the consequences of fire. If there was an in-flight fire, especially in the wheel well, and an upwards firing escape hatch was jettisoned, the resulting vacuum would cause smoke and fire to be drawn violently into the crew compartment through the ladder opening, like a giant chimney. The basic flight crew manual Dash One stated emphatically: "WARNING. The jettisoning of an upward escape hatch prior to the egress of all lower deck members and extra crewmembers could seriously hamper their escape." But if there were a fire on board, it would probably be considered an emergency, not a controlled bail out.

If it was an emergency bail out of course, there was no preferred sequence, just get out. It was every man for himself, as quickly as possible. The command to bail out would be given by the pilot two ways: by interphone and a two inch bright red ABANDON light at eye level on the panel in front of each crewmember. There was also the highly popular but unwritten rule that if you ever saw the pilot eject you had permission to leave.

When each member of the crew went through their bail out class back in flight safety training, they were taught the main thing was: don't touch the yellow handle until you are ready to leave the airplane. In fact, anything painted yellow and black had something to do with your own personal safety. The instructions were split into two groups—upper deck and lower deck. First the upper deck: If you were in an upward firing ejection seat, the magic handle is a six inch by seven inch yellow and black metal frame on the end of the arm rest. Its release is imbedded in the top of the metal frame. Squeeze it and the frame will rotate upward into your hand and several things will happen all at once: the seat is armed, the firing trigger flips into position, the hatch is released into the slipstream, your work station stows itself, (control columns for pilots and gunner, table for EW), and your shoulder strap inertial reel locks. The firing trigger itself does only one thing, it fires an explosive charge into a cylinder that will catapult your ejection seat up and outside, sort of like a very large potato gun.

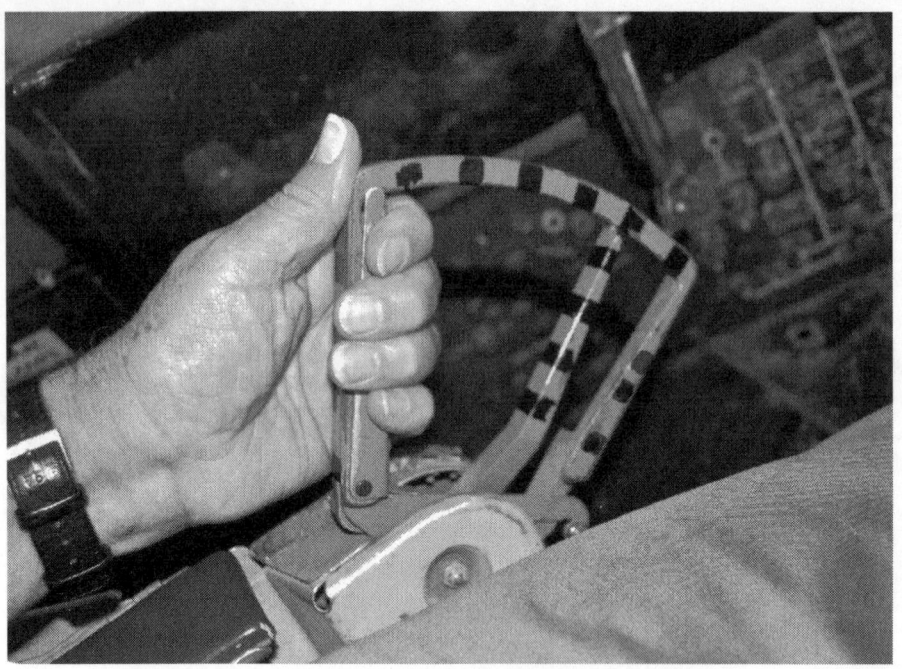

The Ejection Seat Trigger: Magic Handle.
Image by author

Downward ejection seats for the two navigators on the lower deck worked basically the same way, but the yellow D trigger was between the navigator's legs at the front edge of the seat. Downward seats don't have armrests. Holding tightly onto the trigger ring keeps the navigator's arms from flailing around on the way out. Plus, there were ankle restraints that rotated around your ankles and tucked them in. Moving your feet back against the spring-loaded triggers activated the ankle restraints. Every new BUFF navigator triggered these restraints many times during normal flight before he learned not to bring his feet so far back under his seat—unless he's serious about ejecting, of course. When ready to eject, pull the yellow D trigger up in a continuous motion. That would rotate two paddle-shaped leg guards up and around your hips into position beside the thighs to keep the legs tucked in. That was to force your legs inward to be narrower than the width of the hatch opening. The continued pull of the trigger would release the hatch below your feet, arm your seat, lock your shoulder straps, and fire the ejection seat.

When the hatch is released and is carried away by the slipstream, you are reminded there is nothing beneath your feet but air, and that all this time you have been sitting in a seat on rails, not unlike that of the dunking booth at the county fair. And you are the guy in the dunking booth chair.

For any of the ejection seats, either upward or downward firing, one second after you eject, your seat belts will release; a small explosive-powered reel in the seat back will quickly tighten up the two nylon straps that you are sitting on, and you will be flipped away from the ejection seat and your parachute will automatically open. Your seat cushion is still attached to you. It is your global survival kit, containing, among many other things, a rubber life raft. As you are floating down beneath the parachute canopy, the survival kit will fall away automatically and it will stream out sixteen feet and inflate the rubber life raft, just in case you come down in water and need something floating nearby. The earth's surface is 75 percent water, so the odds are three out of four you will get wet. The survival kit and raft will hit first and hopefully reduce your landing weight. If you were sure you would not need the raft or anything else in the survival kit and it was in your way, there was a way of releasing the string of tethers. But you needed to be sure, for the kit did contain a lot of needful things including medical supplies and a firearm, a fold-up .22 caliber rifle suitable for small game hunting, just in case you are out in the bush somewhere long enough to get real hungry.

There was also the possibility that you might need to get out of the airplane in an emergency without using the ejection seats, such as in a crash landing, where the upward firing ejection seats could not carry you high enough for the parachute to function. If you were on the bottom deck, downward ejection was certainly not an option. In that situation, where the airplane was already on the ground (or water), the four crewmen on the top deck would pop their hatches off, throw a rope out, and climb down. Those on the lower deck would go up the crew ladder to the top deck and climb down one of the four outside escape ropes. Sometime after 1961, a warning was placed on the cloth bag that held the escape rope beside each hatch: WARNING. DO NOT HOLD THE ROPE END AND JUMP. The story behind the need for that warning would probably be interesting. It could have been that the rope was longer than the fall distance.

The emergency hatches on the B-52 did not *blow*. When activated by the ejection seat trigger for an in-flight emergency, six latch clamps would rotate out of the way and two small gas cylinders would push the leading edge of a lifter into the slipstream, where it would be carried away, taking the hatch with it.

Winston Churchill once said there was nothing like the fear of being shot at that clarifies the mind. The instant before you release the hatch and hurl yourself into space there is nothing like visualizing the open space directly beneath your feet or above your head to clarify the mind. But then, in an emergency, the training takes over and you probably won't even think.

As they proceeded northward over the North Carolina countryside, Keep 19 descended to ten thousand feet and did an emergency lowering of the landing gear with all the normal gear circuit breakers pulled. They had asked the Command Post for the best altitude to lower gear with the less chance for a spark igniting the fuel. After the landing gear reached the down and locked position, the gear handle was put in the down position and all normal gear circuit breakers were reset. They had just passed a major test: getting the landing gear down without blowing up.

Keep 19 was still under Raleigh Radar control, and they were being directed in from a point forty miles south of the base. The Command Post wanted the crew to activate the airplane's flaps to check out the aircraft's control in the landing configuration, with both landing gear and flaps down. In combat, the rule had been to never lower the flaps if you had a damaged wing. But here, the experts on the ground "must have decided the wing was OK, and our only problem was the fuel leak." Flaps are essential for landing at that heavy weight, but timing was going to be a factor, and they could not wait until final approach to see if the flaps worked. The situation did not seem so critical, as they thought the main tanks had drained themselves.

Major Tulloch began to slow the airplane. The tension of the crewmembers would be at a peak, for they knew they were now going to attempt a night landing with a wounded airplane that had been leaking a whole lot of fuel. Mattocks was helping the pilots with circuits located on the overhead panel behind them that they couldn't reach. They wanted to shut off anything electrical that was not essential to landing. He would also be leaning forward between the pilot and copilot, searching for runway lights. Wilson and Barnish would be twisting around in their backward-facing seats, trying to see down the narrow passageway and out the cockpit windows up front. The two navigators down in the Hole also didn't have any way to see outside. They would have put away loose objects and cleared their writing tables to remove any obstacle between themselves and the downward ejection routes. If they had to eject, the spring-loaded table would snap forward into a slot in the panel in front of them and anything on the work table at that time could make for a nasty airborne projectile during ejection. Major Eugene Richards, behind them in his small jump seat, could only listen in on his headset to the events unfolding beyond his control. In the event of a bail out, he would at least be the second man out, diving through the hatch opening made by the navigator, Captain Paul Brown, a few feet to his front.

After Raleigh Radar turned Keep 19 over to Seymour Johnson Approach Control, Major Tulloch ordered the flaps down as requested by the Command Post. They were at nine thousand feet. It takes the massive thirty-foot wide flaps a full minute to reach the extended position. Just as the flaps started down, he was instructed by Seymour Johnson to turn left from the current heading of 320° to a heading of 260° to line up with Runway 26. This is a heading change of sixty degrees, somewhat sharper than similar intercepting turns for civilian aircraft. It is possible that Major Tulloch may have preferred a more gentle turn, starting much further away from the runway. Now there he was, doing a banking turn to the left, with his right wing higher than the left. But the turn was completed without any control problems, and the final heading of 260° would be later confirmed by Raleigh Radar and witnesses.

They were on a very high, very long final approach. A radio message from the base would have sounded like this: "Keep 19 Heavy, Seymour Johnson Approach. Cleared for the ILS, Runway two-six. Altimeter two niner niner six. Advise the runway in sight. Good luck, sir."

"ILS for two-six. Keep 19," Tulloch acknowledged.

The "good luck" comment would have been a courtesy offered by the Seymour Johnson approach controller to an aircraft in trouble. It was to let the pilot of the landing B-52 know that this was indeed being considered as an emergency, that firefighters would have been notified and were rolling to their pre-assigned positions, and the airport would be closed to all other traffic. Keep 19 owned the field.

During flap extension, the speed reduced from two hundred and twenty to one hundred and eighty knots. The landing gear was already down and locked. Adam Mattocks said that the turn was completed and the aircraft was flying straight and level. Tulloch did a quick check of the indicators. Stabilizer trim zero; rudder trim, approximately zero; airbrake, position two. Flaps indicator showing 100 percent. Then . . . there was a loud noise from under the airplane like it had struck something and there was a violent jerk to the left. The pilots got the plane leveled but then a worse noise came from below. The right wing dropped slightly and the aircraft began a turn to the right. Adam Mattocks thought then and now that somehow the lowering of the flaps during the turn had jammed the control surfaces of the right wing, damaged from the huge fuel leak. Major Tulloch tried to correct this unexpected right turn . . . The turn increased . . . He and Dick Rardin had both the yokes hard left, both were stomping hard on the left rudder pedals, trying to stop that turn . . . Major Tulloch yanked off all power to the four engines on the left wing, and increased power to full on the remaining two outboard engines on the right wing. The big aircraft did not respond. Six of the eight jet engines were either spooling down to idle or already idle on a heavy aircraft with landing gear and flaps down. Major Tulloch was running out of airspeed. He was doing everything that nineteen years of flying had taught him—all his skills, his hundreds of hours of combat, everything he knew—he was putting up the fight of his life and that of his crew. It was coming down to this one instant in time; his hands were flying over the myriad of throttles and controls. Get the nose down to pick up airspeed . . . airspeed coming back up. Worry about heading later . . . looking good. Just maybe . . . Then, there was a loud cracking and thumping noise and the aircraft began an uncontrolled barrel roll to the right. A loud explosion was heard. The right wing was folding up. "The beast was rolling over on her back."

Adam Mattocks had recently gone through a session as pilot in the ground training simulator, where the instructor had set up the exact same configuration: an approach to landing, gear and flaps down, six of the eight engines out, and loss of airspeed. Adam crashed the simulator every time.

He had also, just the day before, gone through in the same simulator the exact steps he would make in order to leave the instructor pilot's jump seat on the top deck and bail out of the opening in the lower deck. He knew it would take him a lot more than the few seconds like the others in ejection seats. While the airplane was starting this last, fatal maneuver, he put into action what he had practiced. First he unplugged his headset, for he did not want to be connected in any way to the airplane. He kept his hand on the belt release. Then he turned in his seat to his right as far as he could, to be in a better angle to his route of escape: the ladder behind him to the lower deck. While mentally preparing for what was to come next, he quickly realized he would not be able to hear the bail out command over his headset, so he quickly plugged back in. That command came immediately from Major Tulloch,

"Bail out!" Amazingly, someone answered back on the interphone, "Did you say bail out?" "Yes!" shouted Major Tulloch, "Bail Out!"

Mattocks simultaneously disconnected his headset and his seat belt and immediately was flung to the floor, on his knees, facing aft. He blacked out from incredible g-forces. He said he thought he was out for two or three minutes, but it must have been only seconds. When his vision returned, he was somehow facing forward, and he saw Major Tulloch, while fighting the violently shaking controls, turn his head and look back at him. He said that look between them agreed on one thing: Adam Mattocks was a dead man. Scott Tulloch's eyes sent the worried message: "I'm sorry . . . " Adam nodded his head as if to say, "It's OK." Then the copilot, followed quickly by the pilot, ejected—each departing like a small, savage, single-passenger rocket ship, a loud bang, but without flames. Mattocks knew he could not make it to the lower level, so he tried something truly desperate. He tried to jump straight out the open overhead right-hand hatch . . . but due to the aircraft's spin actually went out the opening on the left. He was hung up, with only his head and shoulders out. Then it was inertia, or something, that popped him outside the aircraft, stationary, with no wind sounds. He and the aircraft were momentarily suspended together in a bizarre ballet in space, forward motion ceased by the huge wing surface, which was now vertical, instead of horizontal, and was acting as a big air brake.

We know that when Major Tulloch gave the bail out command the aircraft was in a nose down position and had rolled to the right past 90° of vertical, with the tail forward of the nose. The aircraft could not survive this incredible attitude. "Complete aircraft breakup occurred at this time," three hours and six minutes after the crisis began. The right wing broke off, the fuselage cracked in the middle, and the two thermonuclear bombs fell out of the disintegrating, crumbling, exploding aircraft.

Total flight time was thirteen hours and thirty-nine minutes. It was thirty-five minutes past midnight, 0035 hours, January 24, 1961.

"Night Scene Over Faro, North Carolina: The Crash of Keep 19"
Illustration by author

Chapter 3

The Bail Out

Lieutenant Bill Wilson, electronic warfare officer, said that in the minutes before the crash, "There was a lot of chatter going on. The next thing I knew, they said bail out. I took their word and bailed out." He said he told himself, "This can't be happening to me. It's all a dream. When I looked up and saw the chute open, I knew I had it made." When he ejected, his ejection seat separated from him and his parachute opened as advertised. But on the way down, the life raft somehow inflated early—even before he released the survival kit—tangling him in the rigging. He found himself fighting with a boat in midair. He was able to cut the lanyards and free himself before reaching the ground. The inflated life raft quickly blew away in the wind and was never found. Somewhere in North Carolina, a hunter or farmer has probably been surprised to find a rubber life raft, miles from the ocean.

Lieutenant Wilson landed in a plowed field of soft mud. He said later, "I don't know how it happened. I know that when I landed in the field I felt awfully good. I felt like running." Then he thought he saw a bull. He thought it started chasing him in the dark, so he ran to a fence and jumped it, breaking his ankle in the process. He limped to a nearby house, where the owners started a pot of coffee on the stove, and a Mason jar of clear 'medicinal spirits' was made available. "They thought at first I was a prowler when I told them I had jumped out of an airplane. I must have been bad-looking." His broken ankle would prove to be the most serious of the injured survivors. Adam Mattocks, told me in his interview, "Bill Wilson was from New Jersey. He didn't know a bull from a cow. It was an old cow."

When Major Tulloch ejected, the plane was rolling over and he was hanging suspended by his seat belt. There was a gap between him and his ejection seat, and when the catapult fired, it slammed hard against his body. He found himself tumbling out of control, losing his oxygen mask and helmet. He said it was like being inside a big wave at the beach, being overpowered. His parachute opened and he was surrounded by flaming pieces of wreckage as he was coming down. He would say later it was a fine physical sensation, this floating, and he could see why people would do it for sport. He was probably already in shock from the blast of the exploding aircraft. He found himself floating down alongside someone, and found out later it was Gene Shelton, the radar navigator. Tulloch called out, talked to him, but got no response from the limp form. Tulloch came down in a swamp and was hung up in a tree. He could not see clearly in the dark, but he thought he was only a few feet off the ground, so he released his parachute harness. The drop was over twenty feet into the cold waters of the Nahunta Swamp. Shelton was nowhere to be seen. The wind was very strong and they had separated during the parachute fall of over a vertical mile. He was thinking surely that all the boys had gotten out; he could hear the seats firing off before he ejected. When he first heard the muffled explosions he thought it was more trouble, but then he heard the shell that fired the copilot's seat and realized that was a good sound—"The lads were firing their seats off and were safely away."

He was alone in the dark swamp and could see no fires or house lights, so he checked himself for broken bones, took a reading on the North Star, and started wading out of the swamp. But each direction he tried he encountered deeper icy water. He blacked out several times and once found himself face down in the water.

He had flown every bomber in the Air Force inventory during his career, from B-17s to the B-36 to the B-52. He had flown thirty-one combat missions over Japan in B-29s. It would be ironic, he thought, to survive an exploding B-52 only to drown in a swamp. That might be the way his fellow pilots would remember his demise: "Tulloch got out of the plane OK, but he came down in a tree, fell out of it, and drowned in a swamp."

He decided this would be a good time to get out of the water and just wait a bit.

Part of the parachute was hanging within reach, so he pulled on it, and retrieved the orange and white cloth from the tree. He spent the rest of a cold, wet night wrapped in it, teeth chattering, waiting hours for daylight to arrive. For years he had carried with him on every flight a pack of government-issued waterproof matches. Now that he needed them they were lost. He had also lost that often joked-about black eye patch. It was issued to SAC pilots to use when they were going into combat so they would have at least one eye, in theory, functioning after the nuclear blast. He heard rescue helicopters coming over but had no way of signaling in the dark with no flashlight, no matches. He had lost everything from his pockets, things he always checked for, before every flight. He started blacking out again. At daylight he tried moving east, around and away from the deep swamp, found a road and someone picked him up and drove him to a farmhouse with a phone. He called the Wing Command Post to report in, and find out if the rest of the crew made it. His chief concern was Lieutenant Mattocks, for he had been up on the flight deck helping with circuit breakers that the pilots could not reach. Major Tulloch was transported about a mile to the crash site where he "made a dramatic appearance," according to the newspapers. His commander was certainly happy to see him. He was then transported by ambulance to the hospital at Seymour Johnson Air Force Base twelve miles away.

At base housing, Betty Tulloch had been awakened around 6:00 a.m. by the visitation team of two senior Air Force officers and a chaplain. That was the rule: the Casualty Affairs team must be made up of at least two people of equal or greater rank than the service member, along with a chaplain. They were the official notification team, the bearers of bad news. For years, Betty had been expecting them, visualizing in her mind's eye their slow walk up to the door, how they would watch her closely. She knew they would come in, gently ask if anyone else was in the house, and then sit her down. They did all that, but now, somehow, it was all in slow-motion. She was wondering why was it all so slow? She was focusing hard on what they were saying.

They told her the Major's plane had exploded and crashed, and he was missing.

Air Force wives, especially SAC wives, had an unusually tight support group. They knew the drill, and had to get very good at it. Two of her best friends quickly came to be with her, somehow they got the word and just knew to be there. Betty decided not to wake up the boys, Scottie and Andy.

About an hour after she was officially notified that her husband was missing, she got a telephone call from someone at the wing Command Post: "Betty?!—Just a minute—I've got someone who wants to speak with you. . . . Hold on . . . I'm transferring the call. . . . "

It was Scott, her husband, now at the farmhouse. "Why are you crying," he asked, laughing. "Did you spend all the insurance money already?"

Years later the boys would admit they knew what was happening that morning. They were awake, watching from a hiding place and saw all the people and the cars arrive, they saw the gold cross on the chaplain's uniform, and saw their mother quietly shaking.

Betty met Scott when she was sixteen-years-old and a junior in high school in Phoenix, Arizona. He was a dashing twenty-six-year-old Air Force pilot in flight school at nearby Luke Air Force Base, and they met at a

Brethren Church social function. They dated some, on and off, nothing serious. A year later he wanted to take her to San Diego to meet his parents. Nothing doing, said her parents. Two more years went by and Scott was stationed at various bases around the country. He would find reasons to fly to Phoenix to see her every now and then. Then he made another request for her to meet his parents, since he was going into combat. He really wanted to see them, and for her to meet them. Finally, her parents agreed she could go to San Diego, but only after extensive late night talks and with the plan of her staying at her aunt's house. Her first inclination that he was serious was when he asked her, "Do you want to make it a honeymoon?" She said it took three years to get her. When they were married on February 3, 1945, she was nineteen, he was twenty-nine.

Scott and Betty Tulloch on Their Wedding Day.
Image courtesy of Betty Tulloch

The tail assembly did not hit Adam Mattock when he jumped only because the tail was not there—it had just broken off.

"I didn't want to open my parachute and have the plane run through it, so I did the count to one-thousand-three then pulled the D ring," he said. When his parachute deployed, big pieces of falling burning debris narrowly missed him. He looked up and saw he had a big, beautiful chute. "Thank you, Lord."

That's when the plane blew up.

The concussion collapsed his chute and he had a streamer. After he straightened out his parachute, he tried to get oriented. He saw two parachutes above him. He was blown over two fields and tracks of woods by the stiff, westerly cold wind and he could see the moon over his shoulder. Then he realized he was coming down in one of the fires of the burning wreckage. He had already prayed twice before, on his knees in the aircraft and then at the open hatch. He knew the Lord was still with him, but if He needed him to go Home, he was ready. Mattocks yanked his parachute riser controls, slid around the fire, and came down right next to a house that he had not noticed earlier. His first hint that he was near civilization was when he saw electrical wires go between him and the lighted horizon. When he landed, he couldn't even do a roll, he just stuck in the mud standing up. He had somehow gotten out of an exploding airplane, without an ejection seat, and now he was just standing there in the mud, staring at the ground in amazement. He gathered up his parachute and walked over to the house where three people were out on the far end of the front porch, looking away in another direction at the fire. They had not seen or heard him land upright in the soft mud.

"When I stepped on the porch I made a little noise and they turned around and looked at me. I said, 'It's just me. I just bailed out of that plane . . . I'm not from Mars.'" This shocked family, jarred awake by the burning wreckage falling from the sky all around them, appeared to be afraid of him, so he took his helmet off. He wanted to show that he was just a man, not a space alien. He told them that he was from Maysville, North Carolina, and he needed their help badly. The mother said they would drive him to the Air Force base, but would have to wait for the brother who had the only car, to return from the store. He did not arrive for another fifteen or twenty minutes. Mattocks sat stunned, on the edge of the front porch, holding his parachute under his arm. Finally the brother returned. The quiet family then drove him to the main gate of the Air Force Base, let him out, and drove away. When he could not produce his military identification, which was ripped out of his jumpsuit by the g-forces, he was arrested by the gate guards. "What! I'm arrested?" Mattocks shook his head in disbelief. The confused and bewildered air police didn't know what else to do, they didn't know anything about a B-52 crash, so they arrested him for stealing government property—the parachute. It was still strapped to his back.

Copilot Captain Dick Rardin also safely ejected. His report would be in true test pilot format, short and to the point: "I could see three or four chutes against the glow of the wreckage. The plane hit ten or twelve seconds after the bail out. I hit some trees. I had a fix on some lights and started walking. My biggest difficulty was the various and sundry dogs I encountered on the road."

He also was driven to the base, where the gate police, who still thought it was some sort of bizarre hoax, apprehended him too. As Captain Rardin was expressing his considered and flavorful opinion to those at the main gate, Mattocks was giving the names of the crew, the time they had taken off, and other details to the guards to convince them that they really were Air Force crewmembers. Then he asked the security police officer in charge to tell the tower, "Go Code Twenty-Seven." That confirmed what the people in the tower already suspected from the sudden loss of communication, and the fact that *Keep 19* never landed long after being cleared for the final approach. They thought *Keep 19* had lost communications, and was still flying around somewhere—there had been no Mayday call. Now they could see a glow on the far horizon, and they knew there was a serious aircraft accident. An accident involving a B-52 bomber carrying nuclear weapons . . . A Broken Arrow.

Broken Arrow: The accidental or unauthorized detonation, or possible detonation of a nuclear weapon, including the non-nuclear detonation or burning of a nuclear weapon; radioactive contamination; or seizure, theft, or loss of a nuclear weapon or component (including jettisoning).

There are other definitions of situations involving nuclear incidents and weapons: *Dull Sword*, a minor incident that could impair a nuclear weapon's deployment; *Bent Spear*, a more significant incident such as a breach of security; *Empty Quiver*, a missing functioning weapon; and *Faded Giant*, a nuclear incident involving a nuclear reactor or other radiological accident not involving nuclear weapons.

Broken Arrow was the most severe, other than NUCFLASH, which was a detonation that had the potential to create nuclear war. The

Command Post launched their part of the Broken Arrow notifications: to SAC, Operations, Wing HQ, Fire, Security, and the Medics. At base headquarters the base Officer Of The Day continued it by calling the first on his list of people in quarters who had the need to know. Each person in the Broken Arrow telephone tree would in turn call more people, and so on. Soon the entire organization would be brought up to speed by the recall alert. Every function on the base that had any responsibility in a nuclear accident or serious incident would cover their duty station and be prepared to meet that responsibility; everyone from base commander, communications, public relations, personnel, chaplains, civil engineers, etc. Even the base veterinarian, who had responsibility of caring for the guard dogs, was part of a Broken Arrow alert, and would be notified through the telephone tree.

Adam Mattocks and Dick Rardin were finally taken from the main gate to the base hospital while the fire and rescue equipment from the base were rolling. The huge fire trucks had been called off the runway and were thundering out the main gate, black exhaust pouring out, toward Faro at their maximum speed, thirty-five miles per hour.

Fifty miles away in Maysville, out in the rural area called Belgrade, Anne Mattocks was pregnant with their third child. She and her extended family had been up all night having a good time, playing cards, and laughing together, girls versus the boys, sisters and brothers. It was a big, happy family. Anne had eight brothers and sisters, and when both parents died when she was two, aunts and uncles raised all the children. She grew up with an aunt near Hatteras, North Carolina, on the Outer Banks. When Anne was fifteen, her aunt began developing heart problems, and started taking Anne to spend time with other relatives near Jacksonville, North Carolina. "My aunt wanted to make sure that I knew the rest of the family." The aunt died two days after Anne's sixteenth birthday.

She went to high school with Adam Mattocks, but they really didn't care too much for each other. Anne said, "He thought he was going to be the high school valedictorian, but *my* grade point average *took him out*! When we both started to college at A&T University, several of us would ride back home to Jacksonville with him. He was the only one with a car."

Early that morning, around 5:30 a.m., her mother-in-law, who lived next door was up preparing breakfast and the biscuits were ready. She came over with the news from the TV that a plane had crashed. An Air Force jet bomber had crashed in "the Snow Hill" area, east of the air base.

They were staring at each other when blue lights appeared outside in front of their house. Soon, a very nervous North Carolina state trooper appeared at the door and told them there had been a plane crash. Adam's sister and brother asked him if Adam Mattocks was in it. "I really can't say, I know that not everyone was alive. I'm just supposed to take you to the air base." Casualty Affairs had decided that because of the distance from the base, it was better to quickly use the state police instead of the personal visit from the Casualty Affairs Team.

"I've got to take a shower," said Anne in a daze. Neighbors from all over were coming into the house. One of them made a very inappropriate remark about how Anne was now going to "get a lot of money." That's when she came apart.

The trooper said, "Now wait a minute. I didn't say anything about your husband being dead, did I?" He was very calm, and got everyone else calmed down. "Let's just get ready and go."

When Anne got in the police car and they pulled out, it seemed like everybody in the community was following in a long string of cars. When they reached La Grange, someone remembered the mother-to-be had not eaten, so they stopped at a fast-food restaurant. The entire convoy pulled in after them. Sitting in the parking lot, the car radio came on and gave the names of the survivors. Adam Mattocks' name was read. There was much rejoicing in that fast-food parking lot in La Grange.

At the base hospital, the doctors and nurses were amazed at Adam Mattocks' miraculous escape, but were watching him very closely for signs of stress and shock. Newspapers would call Adam Mattocks "the luckiest man in North Carolina." He says he should have died several times that night, both in the plane and out. He prayed each time, and he was in a state of peace. But he wanted to see his children grow, to train them. He saw his entire life pass by his eyes. He knows he survived due to one thing: the continuous prayers of his entire family to a merciful God.

Many other pilots and SAC airmen would later say there was no way he should have gotten out of the airplane in that manner.

Paul Brown, the navigator, safely ejected downward and landed in some trees east of the crash in an old graveyard. A Mr. and Mrs. Singleton picked him up and took him to the base. He had some minor injuries and was glad to see Adam Mattocks and Dick Rardin at the base hospital. They were comparing stories, trying to piece together what had happened. The idea of a wing breaking off a B-52 was so foreign to them but they gradually began to consider it in their discussions.

It was not known why Frank Barnish did not use his ejection seat. He may have been thinking back to that very bad experience over Germany seventeen years earlier. He at least could look out of his gun turret on that sunny day. Perhaps he was stunned, covered in jet fuel, strapped into his ejection seat in the dark, thinking about bailing out of yet another bomber. Or maybe he just ran out of time. He had started the ejection process, "press the top lever and rotate the ejection handle upward" . . . the overhead hatch was gone, but the second lever, the seat trigger, was never pulled.

The bodies of Technical Sergeant Francis Barnish of Greenfield, Massachusetts, and Major Eugene Richards, of Toccoa, Georgia, were found in the main wreckage at the edge of Big Daddy's Road. It was later told that after the fire was extinguished, a Faro volunteer fireman named Add Edmundson saw Frank in his ejection seat and covered his son's head with his coat; he didn't want him to see. Father and son stood quietly at the steaming wreckage for a few moments in the smoke and haze of that cold, wet dawn, heads bowed. Frank Barnish left behind three children and a sick wife. Eugene Richards left behind a wife and son.

Adam Mattocks said later he thought that Major Richards had actually gotten out of the aircraft, but was pulled back inside by the same inertia that somehow had helped him escape through the top of the aircraft. The inertia would have forced Richards in the same relative direction as Mattocks within the aircraft, which would have shoved him up against the roof of the lower deck. He would have been very near Major Shelton, the man who was responsible for the safety of the extra crewmembers on board.

The body of Major Gene Shelton was found the next morning two miles away near Bullhead Bridge, caught in a tree, his neck broken. It was later reported in the official findings that he was jerked against his ejection seat when the parachute inflated and after his helmet was lost. It was also in the findings that "surviving crewmembers did not pull down their visors and did not have chin straps tightly fastened."

Gene Shelton, a native of San Antonio, Texas, left a wife, three sons, and a daughter.

When Major Tulloch gave an interview at the base hospital to *The Goldsboro News-Argus* managing editor Eugene Price, he said, "If there was a hero, it was Gene Shelton." He said Major Shelton was apparently trying to assist Major Richards down in the Hole, and delayed his ejection until it was too late.

Major Tulloch had a rough time at the hospital. He collapsed several times, blacked out from the pain and shock. At first they told him that the others were being collected and were in a room down the hall. "I even thought I heard some of them outside my door. Relief and exhaustion helped me to drift off to sleep. The next morning, when I kept insisting that I wanted to see them the doctors told me the grim truth . . . three of them had perished. That next night I was alone with my grief. This loss sorely affected me, and I was stricken with remorse. Why had I tried to save that cursed plane? I had lost three men I loved like brothers. Black despair dragged me down . . ."

The above quotes are from a narrative written by Major Tulloch a few months after the crash. In it he recalls how he struggled within the grip of despair and how his faith helped him recover. His narrative is included in this report, graciously provided by his widow, Betty Tulloch.

Chapter 4

The Crash Site

Billy Reeves was an eighteen-year-old senior at Eureka High School. He spent a part of his school day at the Industrial Education Center, a technical school, where he was rebuilding the engine of the family car, a 1957 Ford. It wasn't a hobby; it was a necessity, for it was the family's only vehicle. He lived with his family on Big Daddy's Road in Faro, a tiny community in Wayne County, North Carolina. He helped his daddy on the sixty-acre farm, which is not a big farm, and it was a tough go. His dad was ill and had asked his son to try to get a part-time job. Billy found one in nearby Freemont, at the Esso station. The Esso was also the bus stop and it had a grill where Billy got the job of cook. He was a hardworking young man. He closed up the station about 11:20 p.m. that night in January and Mr. Saul, the owner, gave him a lift home.

His room was on the south side of their single story, white frame house and it looked out over the flat farm fields and woods. This part of North Carolina was mostly farmland, but also had a lot of woods and a wetlands area called the Nahunta Swamp. Billy got home that night before midnight and went straight to bed. He had already eaten a hamburger that he cooked for himself on the grill, and the next day was a school day.

He had just started to doze off when he heard a noise like he had never heard before. He jerked wide-awake and looked to the south through his bedroom window as his room lit up bright red from ceiling to floor. "I was scared to death. I was looking at the plane when it fell. I saw it hit the ground, and it exploded twice." He bounced off the door frame as he ran out of his room and found his mother, a deeply religious woman, praying. She thought it was "the end of time."

His daddy ran next door to the house of his uncle, William Edmundson. Both his dad and his uncle were members of the Faro Volunteer Fire Station, which was a mile away in the opposite direction from the fire. Everybody was excited and tried to talk all at once. Then they calmed down a little bit and knew that others would be rushing to the station and getting out the fire trucks, so the two men headed straight for the biggest fire, which was just to the south of their houses. It looked like several fires spread out for miles.

Earl and Mary Lancaster still live at the intersection of Big Daddy's Road and Shackleford Road, and Earl was the assistant chief of the Faro volunteer fire department at the time of the crash. Mary saw the plane just as it crashed to the south of their house and she woke up her husband. Earl jumped up and headed out to the fire station, and, with some other volunteers, cranked up both the ancient two-seater fire engine and the tanker truck. That's all they had, but it was time to go with it.

"We could see it clearly, it just lit up the sky. We knew it was a military plane that'd fell," he said. It was the biggest fire they had ever seen. "It was really something."

Volunteer fire chiefs and assistant chiefs had attended safety meetings by Seymour Johnson Air Force Base representatives. They emphasized that the volunteers should try to avoid any close contact with military aircraft fires; they could be in extreme danger. The volunteers should not try to approach the aircraft itself unless further loss of life on the aircraft was imminent, but they were to protect the lives of citizens and their property. The tanker trucks for the rural volunteer stations did not have foam, but contained only water, which could result in disastrous consequences if it made contact with certain chemicals and materials on board military aircraft. They were instructed over the radio that night to fight only structure and grass fires and to hold short of the crashed aircraft until specialized Air Force fire equipment could arrive from the base.

Rudolph Tyndall got a call from a friend that night. "He said, 'Rudolph, I have some bad news. I think a plane has fell on your daddy's and momma's house.' It scared me to death." As he rushed out to Faro, he could see the bright glow from miles away. It was with great relief that he found his parents safe, the house unharmed. But amazingly, seemingly right outside the house, right next to it, flames rose hundreds of feet straight up in the air, a frightening catastrophe. "My daddy said when he looked out the window that all he could see was fire . . . fire everywhere," Tyndall said. "He said he thought the whole world was on fire, and my mama, she said she thought it was the end of the world." The Tyndall's were quickly gathered up and brought to safety, just as helicopters began to land in the field across the road. Tyndall said, "It was amazing. It really was a miracle that this thing happened and no one got killed in the neighborhood."

The safety instructions about not putting water on military aircraft wreckage may not have gotten through to at least one fire station, which had approached the fire from the south. Ellen Tyndall said, "Firemen reported that water behaved like gasoline on the flaming aircraft. They were unable to put out the fire until the Air Force arrived with foam to extinguish it."

The neighbors were very concerned about the Howard's, whose house was just one hundred fifty yards away from the main crash site, especially since George Howard was blind. Mr. and Mrs. Howard were evacuated from the scene by the military. The flames were scorching their house.

There was heavy smoke, the thick smell of kerosene in the air, and burning debris was hanging and dripping from the trees. Forty-five minutes after the crash, another helicopter appeared with a searchlight "as big as a car" and began announcing over a loud speaker for everyone in the crash zone to evacuate immediately. One gentleman dashed outside into the horror of the night and was frightened to the point of losing control of his bowels. He was extremely embarrassed to be caught in the spotlight out behind one of the tobacco pack houses. The spotlight was bad enough, but then a loud voice from above asked if he was all right. Across the road another neighbor opened his front door and his small dog ran out of the house and was never seen again. The people of Faro were out in their yards, twisting around, dazed and dizzy, trying to figure out what was happening to their world.

Billy ran down the road to where his daddy and two uncles (Add and William Edmundson) were at the biggest wreckage. They could tell it was the fuselage lying across the road. His daddy told him to go get the uncle's truck and take everybody in the family to safety at a relative's home, that this was really bad. Billy took off running hard back to the house, avoiding the smoking, jagged wreckage and craters and loaded up the 1946 Ford flatbed. He somehow jammed all five relatives, four of the adults being "good sized" into the cab and began working their way around the back roads to safety since Big Daddy's Road was completely blocked. They would stay at a relative's house for three days without a telephone, hoping the family firefighters were safe. They watched the terrible news about their small community on TV. All the major networks carried the story and they gathered around the television. They couldn't believe this was happening to them. It looked so different when they saw their houses and family members on TV.

Federal Agent Tom Dority had been in his car near the Greene and Wayne County lines on a stakeout, waiting in the dark to catch a moonshiner and shut down his illegal liquor still. Suddenly the sky lit up for miles. He saw a big fireball fall from the sky and knew immediately what had happened. He called Mike Rouse, a journalist for *The Goldsboro News-Argus*. Mike and Eugene Price, his editor, got out to the crash scene at Faro before the military arrived.

Eugene Price said, "It was eerie as hell. Part of the fuselage lay across the road. I was told that one of the crewmen had been impaled on a tree and that a big box was found attached to a parachute hanging from another tree."

Evan Keel was a young college student who lived with his parents in Goldsboro, not too far from the east end of the runway, Runway Two Six. *Keep 19* would have passed very near their house on the final approach to landing . . . had not the right wing folded up and caused the plane to veer off to the north. Evan and his father, Paul, were volunteers at the Elroy Fire Department, where Paul was assistant chief. Late that January night the Wayne County dispatcher had called Chief Farrell Williams and asked the fire department to help look for survivors of a plane crash. They did not know if it was a civilian or military aircraft. Evan, his father, and two others joined the fire chief in his personal car, a red and black 1956 Ford Fairlane, and the five men rushed out Highway 13 over to Saulston then out the Snow Hill Highway.

When they got to the intersection of Bull Head Road they saw helicopters with searchlights off to the west, so now they knew a military aircraft was involved. They moved slowly over the small bridge at Bull Head Creek, windows down, flashlights out in the cold air, shining up in the trees, down into the black water of the Nahunta Swamp. As they moved slowly up a short incline out of the swamp they saw something orange and white in the trees on the left.

"See if anyone's there!" cried the Chief. They piled out of the car just as a helicopter clattered to a hard, fast landing in a nearby small clearing, showering them with dried tree leaves and pine needles, and someone jumped out running. The parachute harness was empty, with straps hanging down. The Air Force man looked it over carefully and said, "Nothing is torn . . . It looks like it was released by the guy who used it. Let's look around for him." They searched the area but found no other evidence.

Based on later information this was most probably the landing spot of Captain Dick Rardin, the copilot, who had somehow gotten a ride to the base and passed the volunteers on the road going the other way.

The group of Elroy firemen drove west toward other searchlights and turned left down a dirt road now called Shackleford Road. They were now out of the swamp and into cultivated farm fields of brown winter stubble. They stopped and looked at a really big object hanging from a huge white parachute in a group of trees. Someone whispered, "What the hell . . . ?" They did not get out of the car this time. Where there had been a lot of talking going on before, at that point the car got really quiet. They thought it could be a bomb, but this thing was huge, bigger than any bomb they had ever thought possible. Maybe it wasn't a bomb; maybe it was some kind of dropped fuel tank? They drove on to the intersection of Big Daddy's Road where they could see fires a half mile to the south. They checked around, flashing their lights around in the trees, but did not see any more parachutes at the small settlement. With the finding of those two parachutes and this big fire they knew they were witnessing something very unusual and very disturbing. People were out in their yards asking each other what on earth had happened? How was it possible for this much fire and destruction to come from the air? Had two airplanes collided in midair?

After about twenty minutes a big Air Force truck appeared, loaded with armed troops. Two men jumped off and set up kerosene *smudge pots*, temporary warning lights. They lit the wicks and created a roadblock with feeble, smoky flames. Evan and the others looked at each other, then they decided to load up and double back down Shackleford Road to search for survivors in the area to the south-east where there were more searchlights. Guards had been dropped off at regular intervals along the road, and one was now at that thing in the tree. In a field nearby they found a long length of metal pipe that smelled of jet fuel, then a hatch cover with a first aid kit still attached, and then a helmet. The helmet had a piece of tape on it that read: Rardin. They waved their flashlights at the helicopters to let them know of the find.

Charles Davis, who owned cotton and tobacco farmland in the area, had been asked by an Air Force major to ride with him around the area in his station wagon. They arrived at the large object on Shackleford Road, hanging vertically by its parachute in a group of three trees and got a good look at it with flashlights. It was indeed a large bomb, and it appeared to be intact, but had spiral marks and scars and had a big dent in its nose where it had driven two feet into the ground. Charles Davis also owned the land on Big Daddy's Road where most of the wreckage from the aircraft fuselage lay burning.

Soon, there were ten fire departments from the surrounding area, ready to go into action if civilian lives or property were in danger. As far as they could tell no one on the ground had been killed or injured, and aside from some minor damage and the scorched Howard house no other houses or barns were involved. Considering the size of the wreckage area of several square miles that in itself was a miracle. State and military police were setting up roadblocks trying to control and quarantine the area. Air Force firefighters in aluminum-hooded suits were now in the middle of the wreckage on Big Daddy's Road, fighting the fire with foam from the big trucks. After the biggest blazes were put out, they went to the volunteers and asked them to pull even further back, in order to conserve the water in the tankers, they were told. But it might have been for far more serious reasons. Specialists with handheld instruments were very concerned, saying they were looking for missing crewmembers, but they were actually looking for the bombs. The Air Force quickly announced that there were two bombs aboard but both were unarmed and had been recovered, that there was no danger.

Actually, only the part about there being two bombs was true.

The Air Force firemen were following the procedure known as *Moist Mop* for crashes of this nature. The first Air Force people at the crash site were the firefighters, wearing the aluminum *hot suits*, working side-by-side with the radiation teams with Geiger counters. Then EOD teams would find and secure any high explosives. These people wore full face masks and yellow coveralls for alpha particle radiation protection. Security forces kept anyone else, including civilian authorities, at least fifteen hundred feet away from the accident site. Red flags marked the boundaries of the site. In later accidents, the color of the flags changed from red to green "due to psychological factors." Even if there were evidence of radiation, teams were forbidden to post the warning signs with the yellow and black international symbol of radiation. "Don't scare the locals" was an edict of *Moist Mop*.

The bomb in the trees on Shackleford Road was secured by Air Force personnel and vital components removed. A quantity of jet fuel was found inside the supposedly sealed bomb case, showing the volume of fuel that showered down in the bomb bay. Later that morning the bomb would be rendered safe and loaded on a truck and hauled away to Medina Air Force Base located outside San Antonio, Texas. That was one of six nuclear weapon National Stockpile Sites, each located deep inside a military installation for an extra layer of security.

A farmer reported that he and his wife had driven down Shackleford Road several times that morning, just looking around, and had seen something white over on the right-hand side of the road. His wife's right side "just burned and burned," after finding out it was a nuclear weapon hanging in the trees.

Throughout the day, conditions changed. Where the weather had been clear, windy, and moonlit at the time of the crash, shortly afterward it grew cold; and blowing snow and freezing rain turned the soft field into mud and delayed recovery efforts. This was the beginning of a winter storm that paralyzed some parts of the state for days. On Wednesday, January 25, the high temperature was 28°, and the low was 10°.

Wreckage was scattered for miles. The tail section and a wing were in an open field about one half mile south of the bomb on Shackleford Road. Another part fell ten to fifteen feet from a family's house. Two of the eight engines were in the woods one half mile east of the main wreckage on Big Daddy's Road. And out in the middle of a plowed field a few hundred feet from an old cemetery was a fifteen-foot-wide crater six feet deep in the soft earth.

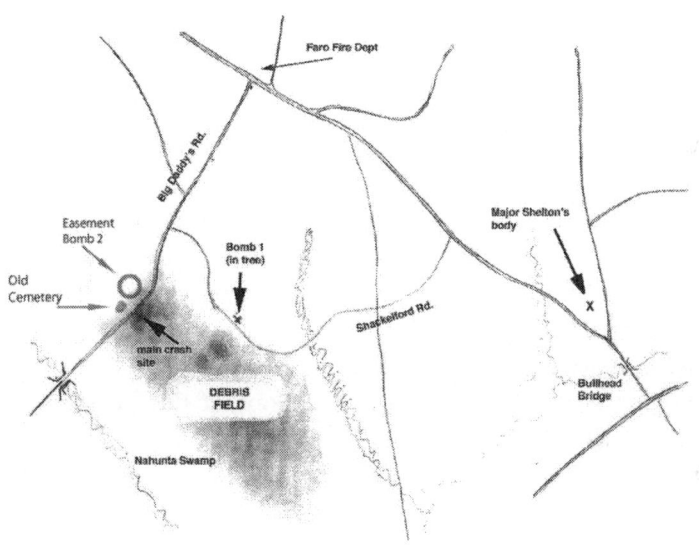

Debris Field, Faro, NC.
Illustration by author

After three days Billy decided that it was time to get the family back home. They had not heard anything from his daddy or uncles. They knew the men had plenty of experience fighting fires; they had to have that skill to protect their homes this far out in the country. Volunteer fire fighting was just something that neighbors did. There were several families around Faro with three generations of firefighters, there still are today. But this was something entirely different, a fire like none had ever seen before. This one was really bad.

Billy loaded up everybody into the truck again; they began to work their way through the woods and swamp, successfully evading the roadblocks, for the Air Force didn't exactly approve of what they were doing. In some places the path seemed barely wide enough for a person, let alone a flatbed truck, but Billy was in his element, he knew the trails. The family was very thankful to make it back safely to their own warm homes and to just be together again. The thanks they said at mealtime took on a new meaning. This had been the most frightening thing ever to happen to them. The night it happened, the Air Force told them, "Leave. Leave. Leave. You don't know how dangerous it is." They left.

For the people around Faro, things began to fall into a routine. They could still smell kerosene fuel, and the aluminum foil countermeasure strips called chaff were still hanging from trees like tinsel. On cold nights with sleet and snow falling, Mary Lancaster would prepare hot coffee for the troops manning the checkpoint in front of their house at the intersection of Big Daddy's and Shackleford Roads. The troops left the empty coffee cups in her mailbox. On several occasions, she saw the change of shift fellows checking the cups in the mailbox for any residue. She quickly offered refills to the new fellows.

At the Buck Tyndall home, a knock at the door came one cold night when it was sleeting. It was one of the Air Force policeman assigned to the road in front of his house. He said, "Mr. Tyndall, we will be spending the night on your front porch out of the sleet, so don't be alarmed if you hear us moving around."

"Son, would you like to stay inside the house?" asked Mr. Tyndall.

"Thank you sir, but we can't do that."

Rudolph Tyndall visited his parents every day to see how they were doing and to help feed the farm animals. He also wanted to check out what was going on in the big field, all lit up by portable lights from Carolina Power and Light. It was amazing. Their house was right beside a crashed B-52 jet bomber and yet the only damage was one cracked windowpane. Digging in the field continued twenty-four-hours a day, seven days a week on the far side of the old cemetery.

Morris Cruise was nine-years-old, one of nine kids, and they lived close to the middle of what was called the debris field, just to the west of Short Road and south of Shackelford Road. When the plane fell, they ran to a tobacco pack house thinking its tin roof would offer more protection from the falling pieces. The rain of metal on the roof was deafening. Amazingly, the debris from the sky hit no one. He saw a wing hit the ground and roll over and over several times. In the morning, they saw an ejection seat in the yard, and it remained there for two days. They were afraid to go near it. They remember finding containers of orange juice and cereal scattered around in the woods, and tasted it. Then they ate some. They found big belts of ammunition and ran around with the ammo around their necks playing soldiers. They had to spend the first night with relatives but were back in their house after that. A big brown tent was put up just to the north of their house, probably the temporary command post. They could see the aircraft's big vertical fin, still attached to the horizontal stabilizer, just sitting out in the middle of a plowed field. It looked so strange, this part of a great big airplane, something so foreign, that had somehow entered their world.

The military asked Billy Reeves to help identify neighbors who wanted to come through the intersection checkpoint near his house. They all wanted to get back to their homes. His mom's specialty for the troops was a mugs of homemade hot cocoa: fresh milk, chocolate, and plenty hot. Schools started back up, and Billy prowled around the area in the afternoons getting to know several of the military people who were guarding the area and searching for wreckage. He and some pals found a metal box of "really big bullets" . . . probably .50 caliber from the four tail guns. He and the others took one bullet each, but the military confiscated them.

Explosive Ordnance Disposal (EOD)

"Jack, I've got a real one for you." The early morning phone call came to the young lieutenant at his apartment in Fairborn, Ohio. His squadron commander was assigning him to the Broken Arrow in Goldsboro, North Carolina. And he was doing it without any of the planned elaborately coded wording that was the official terminology. The phrase, "Jack, I've got a real one for you," cut right to the chase.

Air Force First Lieutenant Jack B. ReVelle was commander of Detachment Four of the 2702nd Explosive Ordnance Disposal Squadron at Wright-Patterson Air Force Base at Dayton, Ohio. His team's job was to be ready at a moment's notice to go anywhere to deactivate anything including the largest thermonuclear device in the world. He and his team usually spent a lot of time at Wright-Patterson doing intensive classified training, along with maintenance of their specialized equipment. Occasionally, they gave assistance to the Dayton, Ohio, fire and police departments acting as the local bomb squad. It takes a special person to be in the EOD: calculating, smart, and able to focus intensely on the task at hand.

Just the previous July he had worked a Broken Arrow adjacent to McGuire Air Force Base, New Jersey, when a Bomarc missile caught fire and exploded in a ready-storage unit, which was also the launch site. The nuclear core of the anti-aircraft missile didn't detonate but the fuel tank fire sure melted it. All of the missile's safety devices functioned as designed, but there was a lot of radioactive contamination from the firefighter's runoff, which was restricted to the immediate area.

ReVelle and his team tried to keep an even balance in their tense jobs. These fellows depended on each other in moments of extraordinary crisis, like any other battlefield brotherhood. A highly unofficial but favorite clothing item was a black tee shirt that had this message printed on the back:

> I AM A BOMB TECHNICIAN.
> IF YOU SEE ME RUNNING,
> TRY TO KEEP UP.

When he got the word about Goldsboro that morning, Jack grabbed his RON (Remain Over Night) kit, which contained a few personal items. He kept the satchel close by him at all times. At the base a two-seat Lockheed T-33 jet aircraft was already warming up and the pilot waiting for his single passenger. On the flight line, Jack hurriedly put on the helmet, which was handed to him and climbed up the ladder and into the rear ejection seat. Two ground crew people were strapping him into the seat parachute harness as another one secured his bag in a small compartment.

"I don't know who you are, or why you need to get to Goldsboro in such a hurry, but I've never been cleared for a *takeoff when ready* while sitting on the ramp," said the pilot, as soon as the intercom was plugged in.

"I'll tell you en route, sir," the lieutenant replied. There was no safety briefing. He had already been checked out in the required aircraft's emergency procedures as part of the job, including bail out procedures and the high altitude chamber training. About an hour after takeoff he was *boots on the ground* at Seymour Johnson Air Force Base North Carolina at 8:30 a.m. Quite a morning's commute of four hundred and fifty miles.

*First Lieutenant Jack ReVelle, EOD Team Commander.
USAF photo.*

Within three hours, and about ten hours after the crash, his team of fourteen EOD technical specialists arrived on a C-54, a four-engine cargo plane. They would be working very long hours in the cold and wet snow. The first task was to safely disarm Bomb Number One, the bomb that came to rest in the center of a clump of three gum trees, which grew wild in a ditch between two cultivated fields on Shackleford Road. The bomb clearly had spiraling marks and scars where it rotated out of the aircraft holding chain when the fuselage broke apart. The chain resembled a very thick bicycle chain that permitted movement only in a one directional plane: down—and held the bomb tightly up against the bomb rack.

Bomb One. MK-39 in the Trees on Shackelford Road.
Image courtesy of USAF

When the *render safe* task had been completed, ReVelle and his team focused their attention on Bomb Number Two, the bomb buried in the plowed field. They began by locating the hole of entry where the bomb had penetrated the ground's surface. The crater was fifteen feet wide and had a center six feet deep. It was 420 feet northwest of Big Daddy's Road, and about 600 feet north of the fuselage wreckage. The team started this initial recovery effort with hand shovels, gingerly removing and analyzing each clump of muddy earth. It wasn't long before they asked for large equipment to be brought in. Eventually very large equipment, such as bulldozers and huge mining draglines, whatever could be rounded up, was used. They did a lot of digging and spent a lot of time down in the dirt over the next eight days.

A Goldsboro civilian excavating company, T. A. Loving, was quickly contracted to bring in heavy digging equipment, and security clearances were required and passes were written. They ended up using two dragline cranes, one cable rig backhoe, sixteen wellpoint pumps, bulldozers, and a lot of trucks. The EOD team needed a wide hole around them and room to work as they went deeper. At 3:45 p.m. on day two, January 25, at twelve feet down in the boggy, sandy soil, they found the remnants of the unopened parachute pack, parts of the nose, and pieces of the conventional explosive which originally surrounded the nuclear core. The HE, or high explosive, was collected in oil-soaked burlap bags and stacked about two hundred yards away.

EOD Team from Wright-Patterson AFB—at Bomb Two Site.
Image courtesy of USAF

One of the people assigned from Seymour Johnson was Airman Second Class Guy Altizer, an Air Force nuclear weapons technician assigned to the 53rd Munitions Maintenance Squadron (MMS.) He had recently finished specialized training at Lowry Air Force Base in Denver. He cared for and loaded thermonuclear bombs on B-52s at the base, and he worked in the field digging through the dirt at the crash site searching for Bomb Number Two. When he worked on his *toys* back at the base, he was not beyond leaving a handwritten message, a little personal note inside a bomb. There had to be at least one other person who knew about the message writing. The *two-man* program applied to the work area; it was a *no-lone* area. No one got near a weapon alone. And no one did anything to a weapon without at least one other person there who knew exactly what the first person was doing. While Guy was taking care of the weapons, he also sanded and painted the bomb casings, just to keep them looking professional. Now he was out at Faro at the edge of the muddy crater with classified documents and the top secret bomb manual. Someone in the hole would wipe the mud off a part and Guy would check off the bomb component by part number and serial number as they were brought up the ladder and identified. That way, they would know which items they had and which were missing.

Jack ReVelle remembers that the Air Force did not have any food service at the site for the first few days. But the Salvation Army was there. From the very start they had hot black coffee and donuts. He still appreciates their service, and makes a significant contribution every year because of what they did fifty years ago at Faro. He said he first learned to drink black coffee from Salvation Army mugs. Guy Altizer said the highlight of his night shift was the hot food served up at the Air Force field mess tent at midnight, available for everyone at the site including the civilian workers. The truck drivers and equipment operators really liked that. Somehow the cold, muddy environment made the hot food taste much better than normal, and there were few if any complaints. There was also a large heated tent with bunks for sleep between the work shifts and for breaks from the extremely cold winter weather.

Over the next several days the EOD team found more pieces of the MK-39 weapon as it peeled apart on the way down through the soil. On day three, they discovered dark water in the hole, not just run-off. Lieutenant ReVelle performed a critical but disgusting test. He tasted the nasty water and found it salty. ("Needs a lot of lemon . . . " he thought.) The salt meant they had hit the water table of the nearby Nahunta Swamp. They had penetrated a peculiar seam of clay that lay over the water level. He said, "We were pumping water out and digging the hole deeper. If we were not able to pump, we never would have found what we did."

The key *tritium bottle* was found intact on day four at a depth of seventeen feet. This contained a very toxic compressed gas that provided boost to the *primary*, the atomic bomb part of the weapon. More essential components were found the following day. When the primary, the volleyball-sized pit of plutonium and uranium, was found; Jack brought it out of the hole in his gloved hands. An Air Force photographer snapped a picture. Jack would later see that picture at the National Museum of

Nuclear Science and History in Albuquerque, New Mexico. He was holding an atomic bomb in his hands.

On day five, Saturday, January 28, Lieutenant ReVelle heard a nervous voice from the hole, "Lieutenant!" ReVelle went down the ladder to Sergeant Lack, who was ashen-faced. "Lieutenant, we've found the ARM/SAFE switch. And it's on ARM!" They were finally able to carefully remove the parachute pack and there it was, right in the center of the firewall. The red triangle with the letter A was very visible.

The attitude of those down in the hole changed some that day. It got a lot quieter. People took time to come up the ladder and stare at the horizon for a while.

Retrieval of Parachute Pack, Bomb Two.
The Arm/Safe switch was found between the two sections of this bomb.
Image courtesy of the USAF

By day seven, January 30, the man-made crater was twenty-two feet deep, fifty feet wide, and seventy feet long. An attempt to wall up the hole failed. The wooden forms could not hold against the shifting of the heavy, wet mud. The only way to dig down more was to dig out more. The hole got bigger.

Security and quarantine became a problem, but not from the local civilians. On one occasion Lieutenant ReVelle looked up out of the hole and saw an Air Force general poking about at the top of the ladder. It was obvious he did not belong there since he was in his *blues*, not muddy fatigues like everyone else. The lieutenant came up the ladder, introduced himself, and said, "General, I will be glad to brief you away from the site, but I think you are putting yourself in harm's way. I strongly urge you to get the hell out of here. You are in imminent danger." He braced for the impact, which did not occur. The general thanked him, told the lieutenant he was doing a fine job, and left.

On the day of the crash, Brigadier General Herbert Loper from the Military Liaison Committee of the Atomic Energy Commission sent a letter to the Joint Chiefs of Staff in Washington, DC. He said that one of the Goldsboro bombs was caught by its retardation parachute in a tree and was recovered, and the other bomb was destroyed by a one-point detonation. The *sealed pit* MK-39 bomb had ninety-two detonators carefully spaced around the high explosive lenses of its spherical surface. If any one of them detonated prematurely it would only set off a lopsided explosion, enough to destroy the bomb and scattering its radioactive contents but would not cause a nuclear detonation. This was referred to as being *one-point safe*.

General Loper's letter on the day of the accident was wrong, possibly in the haste to get notification to Washington. There was no one-point detonation at the Goldsboro site. If there had been it would indicate that a firing signal had reached a detonator, and that in itself would be a sign that the safety interlock system had failed in some way. General Loper wrote the committee a second letter changing his comments from the first. "There is no positive evidence to support the earlier allegation of a one-point detonation."

Then he added, "No high explosives have been found in the crater." Well, maybe at that time there had not been. But Jack ReVelle's EOD crew would remove HE, and put it in "oil-soaked burlap bags" and stack them two hundred yards away from the hole.

Two groups of people from Los Alamos left New Mexico on special C-47 flights and arrived at Goldsboro on Tuesday night after an exhausting eleven hours of flying. One group, called W-7, carried special equipment to test the gas boosting system. The other group, called X Personnel, were made up of men from the Air Force, the Sandia Corporation, and the Atomic Energy Commission. Their report, "W-7-2717" dated February 20, 1961, which is now declassified, identified the two bombs by serial number. This is the first known declassified record of nuclear weapon serial numbers.

Bomb Number One, the parachuted bomb was S/N 434909. Bomb Number Two, the buried bomb was S/N 359943. The Los Alamos people departed Faro on Sunday, January 29, five days after their arrival.

The Air Force had announced they were digging for an ejection seat and asked for the public's cooperation if found. "It is black with yellow arms and has the word 'Copilot' printed on the back." It was not long before local people began to doubt the story about the missing ejection seat. That was a real big hole just to look for an ejection seat. People started to collect and hoard souvenirs so the Air Force made an announcement that they could be prosecuted if wreckage material was not turned in.

Someone said a crane had the bomb in its jaws at one time but dropped it. If this happened it was probably the parachute pack or other components. A complete bomb was huge: 6,750 pounds and eleven feet long. When this one hit the ground without the parachute it was traveling about 700 miles per hour, and components were peeled away as it traveled downward through the soft dirt. The team determined that the weapon fishtailed into the earth. The path was not straight down, but J-curved, and ended with the nose of the weapon pointing slightly upward.

It would later be determined that the aircraft fuselage broke apart between the two bomb bays. The bomb in the aft bomb bay, Bomb Number One (so-called because it was first to leave the airplane), spiraled forward, out of the big bicycle chain that was holding it and out of the broken airplane. That's the bomb that was caught up in the trees by its parachute. It fell the furthest vertical distance, almost two miles.

The second bomb that fell, Bomb Number Two, came from the front bomb bay and fell for 12.5 seconds—about a mile in free fall. Since its parachute lanyard was severed the big chute never opened, and the bomb's 3.5-ton weight quickly brought it up to a speed approaching that of the speed of sound, according to a study group at the University of North Carolina at Chapel Hill.

At day eight, January 31, at a depth of twenty-two feet, the *hole of travel* of the heavy secondary was determined by probe at 1:30 p.m. Two hours later it was determined in a conference, that "based on an estimate of the current situation, the principal hazards were under control and the AMC [Air Material Command] explosive ordnance dispersal support was no longer requested. Remaining operations concerned only the location and recovery of the secondary." The secondary, described by those who know as about fourteen inches in diameter, about thirty-four inches long, and weighing between two hundred and three hundred pounds, had burst through the frangible nose of the weapon and the inertia of its mass carried it further downward into the water-soaked soil. It was not detected by probe down to a depth of fifty feet through the hole of travel. The EOD team from Wright-Patterson packed up their equipment and went back home, and the recovery was taken over by Seymour Johnson Air Force Base EOD.

Nine days after his arrival at Seymour Johnson, Jack ReVelle was back in his Dayton, Ohio, apartment, sitting at his kitchen table writing a letter to his parents. Then it hit him that he had just deactivated two thermonuclear bombs, each capable of leaving a 100 percent kill zone diameter of seventeen miles. At that point his hand started to shake.

Later, a study by the University of North Carolina at Chapel Hill estimated the buried depth of the secondary at 180 feet. Dr. ReVelle says that frequent testing for radiation was done at both bomb locations and no radiation was ever detected.

Digging and pumping would continue for months, but the Nahunta Swamp water just kept coming in through the sandy soil. The sixteen pumps removing six thousand gallons per hour could not keep up.

The issue of *need to know* had always been a point of contention between the military and the public, particularly the press. At the time of the Goldsboro Broken Arrow, the Air Force followed Department of Defense policy and neither confirmed or denied the presence of nuclear weapons in any accident. This was spelled out and later revised, in DOD Directive 5230.16, which basically gave local commanders the right to lie to the public if they felt it was necessary. President Kennedy addressed this at his first presidential news conference on January 25, the day after the Goldsboro accident, and five days after taking office:

"I am anxious that we have a maximum flow of information but there quite obviously are some matters that involve the security of the United States, and it's a matter on which the press and the Executive should attempt to reach a responsible decision.

"I could not make a prediction about what those matters will be, but I think that all of us here are aware that there are some matters which it would not be well to discuss at particular times so that we just have to wait and try to work together and see if we can provide as much information as we can within the limits of national security. I do not believe that the stamp 'National Security' should be put on mistakes of the administration which do not involve the national security, and this administration would welcome any time that any member of the press feels that we are artificially invoking that cover."

> President John F. Kennedy
> First Presidential News Conference
> The Goldsboro News-Argus
> January 25, 1961

"Both nuclear devices have been recovered."

> Captain Jerry Holland
> Information Officer
> Seymour Johnson Air Force Base
> The Goldsboro News-Argus
> January 24, 1961

"We are looking for an ejection seat."

> Captain Jerry Holland
> Information Officer
> Seymour Johnson Air Force Base
> The Goldsboro News-Argus
> January 28, 1961

Major Dick Manley, weapons squadron commander at Seymour Johnson, said that the Goldsboro civilian contractor T. A. Loving provided the dewatering and excavation. That information was confirmed by Jerry Smith who works for the company, and by Donald Robinson, a former equipment operator at the site. The first contract was for a hole 100' x 100' x 20.' When that did not uncover all the bomb components a second contract was made for 250' x 250' x 40.' Soil had to be removed in two steps due to the depth of the hole. A lower *bench* level was dug out twenty feet below the surface to support the initial dragline machine. A second dragline at the top brought up the soil from the bench level, to be spread by bulldozers at ground level.

By February 7 the crater was enormous: over two hundred feet in diameter and forty-two feet deep. It was northeast of the old cemetery, which was left untouched. The cemetery was so old no one knew who was buried there; it didn't have a name and there were no gravestones or markings of any kind. Rudolph Tyndall said he hunted rabbits there when he was a boy and at that time it had old wooden grave markers, but you couldn't read them. By 1961 there was nothing but briars and brush.

The man-made crater had a circular road descending around the edge for vehicles and people. One person said, "The Caterpillars down in the hole looked like toys." Another said, "It looked like they were digging a lake. I have always heard they lost a bulldozer and it's still buried there." At one point there were six bulldozers working the site. Al Yelverton stated, "It was all anyone talked about. The hole was huge, taking up most of the field." Billy Reeves thought the whole area looked like a small city. A total of 93,000 cubic yards of dirt was removed, according to Loving records.

Major Manley remembers that the water in the hole was an unusual aqua blue, and a seam of clay around the hole was a smoky blue. He took samples of the clay to North Carolina State University in Raleigh for chemical analysis. He said he could not tell them what to look for; they just had to report on what they found. He wanted to avoid any mention of the words uranium, plutonium, or radioactivity. The written report said the sample contained bauxite, and was high in aluminum, with traces of iron. The men operating the machines said this layer was common for the area and was called gumbo. It was the consistency of thick modeling clay. It formed an impervious barrier to the water below and when it was penetrated the water level would tend to rise.

The day of the crash Major Manley and another officer were inspecting the wreckage of the fuselage that lay upside down across Big Daddy's Road. In the area where the cockpit would have been they found the melted remains of the pilot's readiness switch, set to SAFE. Major Manley took it along with a spare to use for comparison to the wing commander, Colonel Osce Jones. Colonel Jones asked him if he had a safe in his office. "Yes, Sir," he answered.

"Then put this in it, and don't give it to anyone until I say so." The melted pilot's readiness switch stayed there until Colonel Jones said to turn it over to the Sandia Corporation in New Mexico.

By March 27, two months after the crash, the news had leaked out that the Air Force was digging for a missing nuclear device. At this point the Air Force revised their position and announced formally that they were looking for a harmless part. "All but one inert portion of the weapon has been recovered. The remaining portion is not explosive and there is absolutely no danger from it," stated Colonel Jones, commander of the 4241st Strategic Wing stationed at Seymour

Johnson. The news was accepted at the time, but in later years the wording was reexamined.

The flooding at the crater was now uncontrollable and the high water table made further digging impractical and unsafe. The Raleigh Airport reported that eighteen inches of rain fell in the area between January and May of 1961. The USDA Soil and Water Conservation Service say that the water table in the Faro area typically averages only one and a half feet below ground surface at that time of year.

Digging was halted on May 25, four months after the crash. The hole was filled in, finishing up in July. Convoys of heavily loaded flatbed trucks lined the roads from Faro heading back to Goldsboro. A study group at the University of North Carolina at Chapel Hill calculated that based on the weight and shape of the bomb, with the impact angle, velocity, and soil composition, the missing component was lodged at a depth of 180 feet, plus or minus 10 feet. The probable minimum estimated cost of recovery was in the neighborhood of five hundred thousand in 1961 dollars.

Much later, when the farmers were allowed to start plowing again, they continued to turn up wreckage of metal and tubing. Years after the crash, people continued to find aluminum foil strips of chaff. Mary Lancaster found a pair of eyeglasses buried in her garden. The plastic earpiece was broken, and they appeared to be military issue. Buck Tyndall's plow snagged on a buried five-foot-long chain that was extremely large and heavy with links about twelve inches across.

*Wing Removal, Moving Down Big Daddy's Road, Faro, North Carolina..
Image courtesy of Mary Lancaster*

When the excavation was filled in, the layers of rich topsoil were put in first instead of on top, according to the farmers. The red clay on top made for poor crops for years. The summer after the accident, Charles Davis answered a knock on his door. An Air Force general had been flying over when he noticed thousands of sparkles on the ground, and he sent out a team to take soil samples. They found recently applied fertilizer pellets shining in the sun.

The Army Corps of Engineers dug another hole north of the old cemetery and many fifty-five-gallon metal drums were buried there, probably containing tons of contaminated fuel-soaked mud and dirt. Any bits and pieces of wreckage itself scattered over the ten square miles of the debris field would have been picked up by Air Force personnel and transported to Medina Air Force Base in Texas for accident analysis.

There has never been any sign of radioactive contamination at Faro.

The government, through the Corps of Engineers, bought an easement of the area for one thousand dollars to prevent digging more than five feet down. Crops could be planted but no digging or drilling was allowed beyond five feet, and "no structures of any kind whatsoever." There is nothing to mark the easement site. Based on the legal description of property records at the Wayne County Courthouse, the center of the 400-foot circle easement would be about 380 feet northeast of the center of the old cemetery on Big Daddy's Road.

The missing component, known as the secondary has never been found.

Crash Site, Then and Now.
By using the location of the Tyndall house and barn in the top photo (taken at the time of the crash by The News & Observer), the location of the bottom photo (taken in 2010 by author), is at the site of the main wreckage. Both photos are looking southwest.

Chapter 5

The Chance of Nuclear Detonation

As human beings it is both our right and our responsibility to insist that the degree of safety in any weapon system be in direct proportion to the fear of danger: the bigger the bomb yield the more safety we want built in. Since the inception of nuclear weapons there have been redundant and elaborate safety systems to insure accidental detonations never occur. One such system in place on *Keep 19* was as simple as pulling on a rope: a cable ran from the crew compartment to bomb bays to allow extraction of safing pins during flight and before the bomb drop. Another system involved rigid arming rods that were removed when the bomb fell away from the airplane. These rods acted like Wile E. Coyote's TNT plunger. When pulled out, the rods generated an electrical pulse that started the fuzing and firing sequence. If the rods were not removed cleanly at bomb drop, the arming process never started. If the plane crashed with the rods in place then the arming process never started. But it is believed this Broken Arrow accident was unusual in a way never before experienced: the B-52 was vertical and breaking apart in midair. This bizarre position and the centrifugal forces from a spinning airplane allowed the departure of Bomb Number One to simulate in some ways a true weapons release.

The Sandia report stated in their after-crash investigation of Bomb One: "There was no scoring or other physical damage to the assembly which would indicate that any unusual forces had been applied. Also, since the holes for the safing pins were not in any way damaged, it must be assumed that the safing pins were extracted prior to separation of the weapon from the rack."

Bomb Number Two, from the forward bay, also had clean rod removal. But the parachute static line, which was attached to the aircraft, was torn away and did not release the parachute, which in itself stopped the arming process of that bomb. But what was found later in the hole in the ground at Faro in the wreckage of Bomb Two, caused serious questions to be raised about the reliability of the safety devices on nuclear weapons.

According to the Sandia report of component behavior (Appendix D) in both bombs, the arming wires were pulled, which activated the pulse generators; the explosive actuators fired, and inside the falling bombs, timers started and ran, the barometric switches engaged, the low voltage batteries were actuated, and contacts closed. But one very important device, the ARM/SAFE switch, at least on Bomb One, was still in the *safe* position. That one device was considered the gold standard of safety; there was no way that either bomb could detonate with that switch on safe.

The very industry that created the switch would later examine that view more closely.

The government classified both of the 1961 Goldsboro bombs as *unarmed*. This should not be confused with the bombs being incapable of nuclear detonation. The arming of the bomb is a series of several steps. Chuck Hansen, who was a highly respected civilian nuclear historian said, "It was like a fully loaded pistol with the safety off, and the hammer cocked—it is not armed until the final safety mechanism, the trigger, is pulled."

Hansen considered both bombs to be unarmed but nuclear capable.

Later, according to then Secretary of Defense Robert McNamara, the first bomb to leave the aircraft, the bomb caught in the trees on Shackleford Road, had "all but one of the arming devices engaged" and in his opinion was extremely dangerous. In a 1983 press conference he said: "It ran through six or seven steps in order to detonate and it went through all but one, we discovered later."

Were these two statements by Hansen and McNamara alarmist? At least now we have the luxury of viewing events from a historical standpoint. It has been better said of the fully loaded pistol statement that the ARM/SAFE switch was in fact, the pistol's safety, and it was ON, and that any attempt to fire the pistol never got beyond that point. If the trigger was pulled it was to no avail.

However, as gun owners know, even a loaded pistol with the safety on can sometimes fire if dropped. Remote, but possible.

It is bizarre to visualize Bomb One, this huge 6,750-pound bomb, suspended by a parachute caught up in a group of trees with its nose stuck two feet in the ground. We now know that the trigger of this bomb is ground contact, provided that all safeties were satisfied. The Mark 39 Mod 2 had a specially designed *crush nose* switch, two metal plates separated by an air space. Other types of nuclear bombs could be set to detonate at a certain altitude after the drop. This one would only detonate when it made contact with the ground and one metal plate touched the other. There was the option of timers, which would allow the *laydown* configuration, but it was the nose contact switch that initiated detonation. That's one reason why it had such a big parachute, to insure a controlled speed and to aid the fins in proper orientation for ground contact.

The other reason is to allow time for the bomber crew to escape the zone of destruction.

If the ARM/SAFE switch prevented detonation of the first bomb, then detonation of the second bomb "may have failed because it apparently was a dud," at least those are the words that were used by Ross Speer of the Atomic Energy Commission. The second bomb, the buried one, essentially destroyed itself as it traveled down through the wet soil at high speed. At first they thought that process stopped all chances of nuclear detonation. But Mr. Speer, the official accident observer, gave conflicting information in his report. At one point he said, "We wondered why bomb No. 2 had been a dud . . . Electrically, the MC-772 (ARM/SAFE) switch proved to be neither in the armed or safe position." Some people have interpreted this somewhat ambiguous report as Mr. Speer being shocked that there had *not* been a nuclear detonation upon ground contact.

A letter from Airmunitions, Ogden Air Material Area, Hill AFB Utah, said, "On the 28th of January, the Arm/Safe Switch of Bomb 2 was revealed and found that it was in the 'Armed' position, and the Low Pack had been energized." Other reports referred to it as "armed but damaged."

What we need is a summary about the possibility of detonation of the bombs at Faro. Lieutenant Colonel Wilton Strickland, USAF (Retired), a former radar navigator on B-52s, wrote this one:

> The internal switches in the fusing and firing systems for both bombs did not fail. They worked exactly as designed. Pullout switches and rods for both bombs were extracted during departure from the aircraft, initiating the fusing and firing sequence. The parachute static lanyard for bomb #1 was still connected to the aircraft, causing the parachute to deploy automatically and allowing the fusing and firing sequence to proceed in the normal, planned manner, including production of a firing signal when the nose was crushed upon impact with the ground. Action of all of these switches was irrelevant, though, and there was no nuclear detonation, because the bomb's internal ARM/SAFE switch was in the SAFE position.

The parachute lanyard for bomb #2 had been torn from the aircraft prior to the bomb departing the aircraft, therefore, the parachute did not deploy. Without the retardation chute, the bomb fell very fast, struck the ground 2.5 seconds before the fusing/firing sequence could complete, and destroyed itself and the fusing/firing system upon impact. Though the internal ARM/SAFE switch appeared at the crash site to be in the ARMED position, later analysis proved that the indicator had been rotated by impact damage, and the internal contacts were, in fact, still in SAFE position. Bomb #2 failed to yield a nuclear detonation, then, for two reasons: the parachute failed to deploy causing fusing/firing sequence to be halted by impact damage and the <u>internal</u> component of the ARM/SAFE switch actually stayed in SAFE position.

Back at the Laboratory . . .

This was really a whole new Broken Arrow scenario because of the way the airplane came apart in midair. There were enough troubling elements in the weapons behavior that Sandia Corporation and the entire weapons industry began an intense decades-long analysis. Sandia is still the Queen Mother of nuclear weaponry and this incident was at the rise of their reign. They were the premier US nuclear facility for twenty-five years, and 1961 was right in the middle of those years. Their analysis Number NND 922015-99 declassified June 18, 2004, showed that, indeed, the "safing pins were extracted from the Bisch generating action rods, and the rods themselves were extracted from the pullout assembly. On both weapons the fuzing sequence was initiated." The key that prevented detonation of Bomb No. One, the report maintained, was the internal component of the ARM/SAFE switch remaining in the safe condition.

Here's a thought: If the switch of Bomb Two appeared to be on ARM, but the contacts were really on SAFE, could the reverse also be possible? Just for the argument, could the switch appear to be on SAFE, but the contacts really be on ARM? And if so, how could the device with such a lofty pedigree, i.e., the Sandia *gold standard*, be so ambivalent in its sole purpose?

Such troubling elements created another gnawing worry about one more critical aspect of the switch: the fact that electrical solder melts. A 1998 study by Sandia Labs (Plummer and Greenwood, "SAND-98-1184C," 2) said that:

Elaborate computer models and fault trees were generated to calculate the probability of an inadvertent detonation [at Goldsboro]. Although the analyses became increasingly sophisticated, did they assure safety? The models focused on the weapon response to a single environment. How could the effects of credible combinations of abnormal environments be addressed?

The methodology above suffered from a fatal flaw. There was no technical basis for some of the underlying assumptions. In fact, some were grossly misleading. For example, a fault to ground may not dud the system at all. It may simply create additional propagating damage leading to further unpredictability. The fundamental problem was expecting the accident to manufacture a 'safety device or feature' from charred insulation or melted solder instead of deliberately engineering these responses.

The experiences of the 1950s and the 1960s taught [weapons] designers some important lessons. First, accidents frequently mimic the delivery mode of the weapon. How is a bomb to know if it was deliberately or inadvertently released from an airplane? Second, wire insulation and printed circuit boards become unpredictable during a fire and it becomes relatively 'easy' to get a 28 VDC across the terminals of a safety device.

In trying to visualize how all this works, it helps to know about the first thermonuclear test, and how lightning was created in a bottle: an eighty-two-ton, twenty-one-foot-tall bottle. As part of Operation Ivy, the MIKE test occurred on November 1, 1952, at Eniwetok Atoll in the South Pacific. This birth of thermonuclear detonation was analyzed by the use of five *hotspot light pipes*, tubes several miles long and absolutely level. These five pipelines carried neutrons and gamma rays from locations inside the device itself to measuring instruments in distant blockhouses as they were being vaporized. The scientists could actually see inside the bottle as it went thermonuclear. Also, a new phenomenon called *bomb light* was captured by a semicircle of seven mirrors sending images two miles to turbine-driven streak cameras. The cameras operated at the incredible speed of 3.5 million frames per second.

The Sandia report came to the position that (a) some previous assumptions were grossly misleading, and (b) it was at least theoretically possible for electrical current to actually jump from one contact switch point to another in the molten solder of an aircraft flash fire or explosion, *even if the switch itself was on SAFE*. This may have been the weakness of the ARM/SAFE switch that so concerned Secretary McNamara in his 1983 news conference. This possibility of safety device failure, although remote, was important enough that the weapons controls industry would study that possibility, and would make enormous capital investments in new and different strong-link/weak-link safety systems, systems which would further reduce the chance of accidental detonation while at the same time promoting reliability as a viable weapons system.

The physicists and engineers at two locations, Sandia and Los Alamos, were some of the brightest people in America. Los Alamos designed the warheads, Sandia engineered everything else: the firing and fusing sets, the arming devices, the safety devices, even the parachutes. The atmosphere at Sandia National Laboratories in Albuquerque, New Mexico, is best described in Barbara Moran's book, *The Day We Lost the H-Bomb*:

> Sandia in the 1960s was a secret paradise for the slide rule set. Every engineer who worked there had graduated in the top of his or her college class. They had cutting-edge equipment, seemingly endless funding, and a fairly loose rein. They also worked with a deep sense of mission. Nuclear weapons, most of them believed, kept their country safe from the Soviets. Sandia engineers considered themselves to be not only the elite of Albuquerque but indispensable to the defense of the United States.

There was an answer to the question, "Were we safe?" Yes, as long as the ARM/SAFE switch held, and a chance miniature lightning bolt didn't find its way through a splash of molten solder in a millionth of a second; or some other obscure thing happened that we had not even thought about. So the switch did its job, it held. But scientists and engineers are well aware that any machine made by man is subject to failure, and they were working hard and fast to replace that switch with something better.

To answer the question, "What were the chances of nuclear explosion?" you would have to ask just how near to the biggest bolt of lightning in the universe do you wish to stand? Some experts say we were very close to accidental detonation at Faro. Some say there was no way:

we had the switch. We may never know the exact truth, it is somewhere in between.

"How close was it to exploding? You're asking my opinion?" Dr. Jack ReVelle was responding to a reporter at a very unusual appreciation dinner hosted by Randy Gray, the Faro fire chief. It was on the anniversary of the Goldsboro Broken Arrow, held in the Faro Volunteer Fire Station, the very fire station that was first to respond fifty years and two weeks before, and one mile away. Most of the visiting guests had never met before this dinner. There were so many people who wanted to attend that space became an issue, so a second presentation by the author was planned for a week later at a much larger Goldsboro church.

Attending the appreciation dinner at the fire station was Adam Mattocks, the last remaining survivor of *Keep 19*, who escaped from the exploding B-52 without an ejection seat. As the third pilot, he jumped through the open hatch where the pilot had ejected. Also attending was Earl Lancaster, the assistant fire chief at the time of the crash, the first emergency official on the scene about an hour before the Air Force fire equipment from Seymour Johnson arrived. Rudolph Tyndall, whose parents lived in the farmhouse right beside the crashed fuselage, was there. Guests Billy Reeves, Mary Lancaster, and Morris Cruise were all eyewitnesses to the crash, which was close to all of their homes. C. T. Davis, who owns the land of the crash site, and Brent Tyndall, who farmed it, attended. Mike Rouse came; he was the first reporter on the scene. Many people attended who lived on farms in the area and saw the disaster as it occurred; they wanted to know more about what really happened. Guy Altizer attended. He had loaded MK-39s into BUFFs at Seymour Johnson—he didn't know about this actual mission, but he definitely helped dig one up at Faro. Andy Tulloch from New York, son of Major Scott Tulloch the aircraft commander, came to the dinner. And Dr. Jack ReVelle—now a quality control author and aerospace statistical consultant in Orange, California—made the trip. He was the explosive ordnance disposal lieutenant that rendered safe two MK-39 thermonuclear weapons fifty years earlier and one mile away from where he was now being interviewed by newspaper reporters, live TV, and Public Radio.

"How close was it to exploding? My opinion is damn close. You might now have a very large Bay of North Carolina if that thing had gone off," he said.

How Big Were Those Bombs?

The basic measurement of thermonuclear weapons is the megaton, which is the equivalent destructive power of one million tons of TNT. Based on the published photos at the time, Chuck Hansen first identified the bomb in the trees as the MK-39 Mod 2 and later reports confirmed this. This type of bomb was made over a two-year period, from 1957 to 1959, and seven hundred of them had been produced. The MK-39 was retired from service in 1966.

It had three parachutes, packed in a series. A six-foot drogue chute was pulled open at bomb departure by a fixed nylon static line attached to the aircraft. The drogue would then be released and take with it a cloth bag surrounding the twenty-eight-foot stabilizing ribbon parachute. The ribbon configuration was to absorb the shock of a high-speed opening. After slowing the bomb to the proper speed, the ribbon parachute would cut loose. This in turn would release the third chute: the big retardation parachute, a one-hundred-foot-wide, ivory-colored monster, believed to be the biggest parachute in use at that time. That size was necessary to support the 6,750-pound weight of the bomb. The bomb was eleven feet long, thirty-five inches wide at the middle, and forty-four inches at the tail section. It was designed in three configurations: air burst, ground contact, and laydown. The laydown modification was just that—it would lie on the ground for a designated length of time and then detonate. One story told of a message stenciled on the outside of a laydown bomb in Cyrillic: "Hey, Dmitry, how far can you run in three minutes?"

The bombs at Goldsboro were Mod 2, set for ground contact.

There were some differences between various weapons charts that are now available; one had the yield of the MK-39 at three to four megatons, while an earlier one had it at two to four megatons. The difference may have been based on different modifications. The yield wording contributed to controversy since two to four megatons somehow became twenty-four megatons in the press after the Goldsboro crash, and that mistake was repeated many times over the years. The error was picked up by others including Dr. Ralph Lapp.

Dr. Lapp was a well-known atomic scientist and the former executive director of the Department of Defense's Atomic Research and Development Board. He was the man who coined the phrase *The China Syndrome*. He published a book, *Kill and Overkill: The Strategy of Annihilation*, the same year of the Goldsboro Broken Arrow—1961. In the book he states that each Goldsboro bomb was twenty-four megatons.

He may have missed a fact in rushing the book to the publisher the same year of the crash. That would have been bigger than anything in the US strategic nuclear arsenal.

Later, while at the University of North Carolina at Chapel Hill for a presentation about the Goldsboro incident, Mr. Hansen stated that he did not believe that Dr. Lapp was being disingenuous with his report of twenty-four megatons, rather it was a simple but very significant misplacement of a decimal point.

In any case, it is no less comforting to know that even a 2.4 megaton bomb would exceed the yield of all munitions (outside of testing) ever detonated in the history of the world—by TNT, gunpowder, conventional bombs, and the Hiroshima and Nagasaki blasts, combined.

Scott Hardy was a graduate student in 2005 at East Carolina University working on his master of arts degree in history. He selected this crash for his thesis research. His thesis was named *The Broken Arrow Of Camelot: An Analysis Of The 1961 B-52 Crash And Loss Of Nuclear Weapon In Faro, North Carolina*. In it, he used the conservative measurement of 2.4 megatons:

> The calculations are chilling. The initial blast itself would have killed only a few hundred people in the rural population of Wayne and Greene counties. But those counties plus Wilson, Pitt and Edgecombe would have had thousands of casualties, including forest and house fires along with terminal burns and fatal radiation poisoning. By best estimates using the 1960 US Census, at 2.4 megatons the bomb would have killed over 3,500 people with total casualties over 66,000…This is not counting any deaths and injuries due to radiation. With a prevailing northwest wind, the radiation cloud would have been carried southeast toward the populated center of Wilmington, North Carolina. The death total would have been in the thousands with ramifications of cancer and birth defects raging for many years.

Dr. ReVelle says that based on the information that he was given at the site the yield of each Goldsboro weapon was 3.8 megatons, and the 100 percent kill zone would have a radius of 8.5 miles, or a diameter of 17 miles. That does not factor in the extreme damages done from the blast outward by base surge and overpressure. Dr. Dietrich Schroeer, nuclear physicist and professor of physics at the University of North Carolina at Chapel Hill, said that this blast from a ground-level detonation would have left a crater in the ground one-third of a mile wide at Faro.

Using these two data points (the one-third mile crater size from Dr. Schroeer and the kill zone from Dr. ReVelle) along with the interactive simulator found at www.MeyerWeb.com/eric/tools/gmap/hydesim.html you can see the effects of a 3.8-megaton bomb if it exploded, say, at the Empire State Building in New York City. I picked that location simply because it is difficult to get a sense of scale at the actual Faro site.

The simulator is based on information in *Effects of Nuclear Weapons, 3rd Edition* by Samuel Glasstone and Philip J. Dolan.

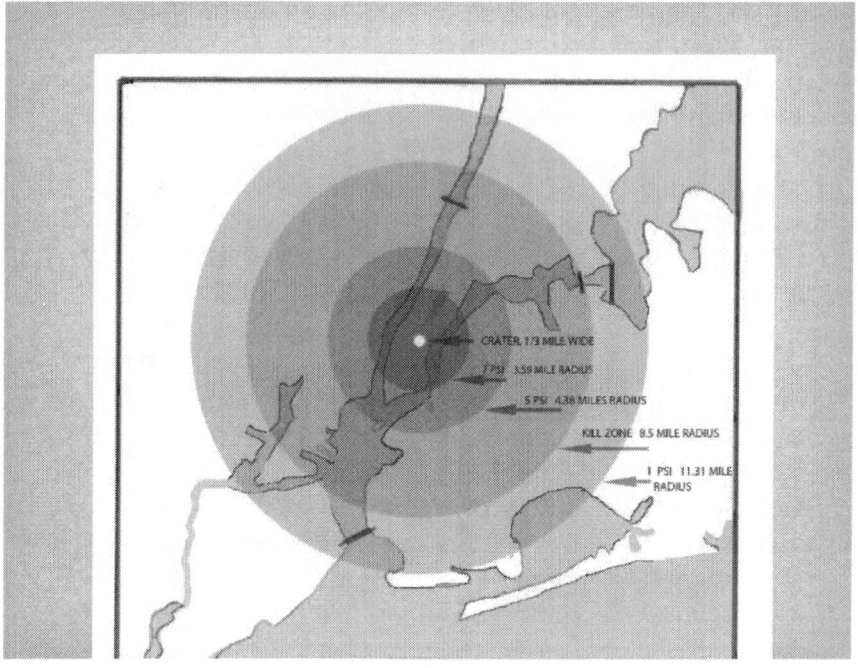

Impact of MK-39 on Manhattan
Illustration by author

Theoretical impact of 3.8 MT weapon, detonated at Empire State Building.
Crater size: one-third mile diameter.

Overpressure Key:

7 pounds per square inch (psi), radius 3.59 miles: Severe damage to complete destruction of reinforced concrete structures, such as skyscrapers, will occur in this ring.

5 psi, radius 4.38 miles: Complete destruction of ordinary houses, and moderate to severe damage to reinforced concrete structures, will occur within this ring.

2 psi, radius 8.5 miles, kill zone: Kill zone of 100 percent of people in the open. (Source: Jack ReVelle).

1 psi, radius 11.31 miles: Light to moderate damage to ordinary houses will occur in this ring.

If we use pure mathematics, one Goldsboro bomb of 3.8 megatons would be about 264 times the destructive power of the Hiroshima bomb. A much different comparison was the 1956 Bikini Atoll test. That was the first airdrop of a live hydrogen bomb and was part of a weapons-testing program named Operation Redwing. The device dropped on May 20 from a B-52 was not a MK-39, it was a TX-15-X1 test device of 3.8-megatons, and the same yield as each Goldsboro bomb. It was said to be "roughly the equivalent of two thousand bombs the size of the Hiroshima bomb." The difference in estimated destructive power from the same 3.8 megaton yield is not explained; perhaps it had a different *boost*, or maybe it was because the Bikini bomb detonated at four thousand feet, twice that of the Hiroshima bomb.

If either Goldsboro bomb had detonated, eastern North Carolina, at the very least, would now have that very large bay or lake that Dr. ReVelle referred to in his interview. After all, the ground surface at Faro is only 108 feet above sea level. In 1977 the Stockholm International Peace Research Institute called the Goldsboro explosion, if it had happened, the "largest man-made disaster in history."

What's In The Ground?

Humans have an inherent fear of the new and unknown, and thermonuclear bombs fit right into both of those two categories.

Thermonuclear bombs contain two types of solid radioactive materials, plutonium and uranium, among others. Another material, called tritium, is in gas form. Plutonium, what some consider to be among the world's most toxic poisons, does not readily exist in nature. It can only be created in a nuclear reactor, and is both a poison and a radiation hazard. It was first *born* about a decade before the Goldsboro crash, but it has a very, very long life. Half-life is the amount of time that radiation will dissipate to half strength. The half-life of Plutonium-239 is over 24,000 years; uranium half-life is approximately 4 billion years.

To visualize what's still in the ground at the Bomb Two site at Faro, you have to make some shortcuts through a complex process. The following is based on declassified information and has some very basic assumptions, but hopefully it will help explain what could have happened fifty years ago and what the area still has to deal with today. Shown below is a representative drawing of what a typical Teller-Ulam device, such as a MK-39 looked like at that time: a large, high-yield design. The two main components of the bomb were a sphere, which was the primary, and a cylinder, called the secondary. The primary stage is basically an atomic bomb that explodes first, creating pure energy plasma that flows around the cylinder shape of the secondary stage while at the same time triggering the plutonium *spark-plug* of the secondary. Fusion fuel is supplied in the form of Lithium-6 Deuteride in the secondary.

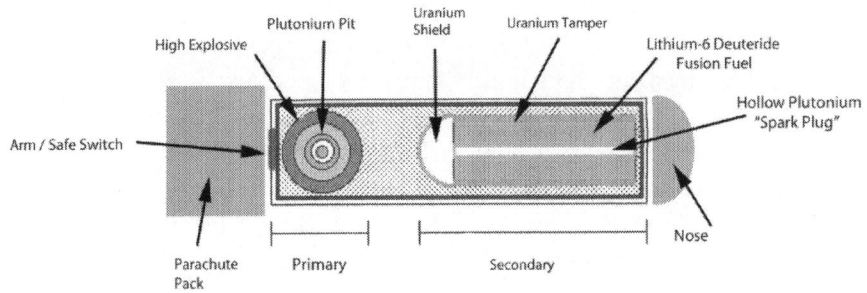

Schematic of MK 39 Type Weapon.
Illustration by author

The exact amounts of plutonium and uranium that are contained in a MK-39 are still classified. What is not classified is other data, including the shape and size of the primary for example. It is about a foot in diameter and has a pattern like a soccer ball around the surface: twenty hexagons and twelve pentagons. This one had ninety-two detonators stuck in explosive lenses all around the surface. When the explosives are fired they compress the plutonium pits inward creating critical mass. We know that the EOD team removed the primary from Bomb Two—Lieutenant ReVelle carried it out of the hole in his shielded hands. That is the photograph in the archives of the National Museum of Nuclear Science and History in Albuquerque.

Getting all those explosive lenses of the primary to fire at exactly the same instant was a very tricky problem back at the Manhattan Project. Most of the scientists didn't think it could be solved because no one had ever used explosives to assemble something before; their normal use was for blowing things apart. Navy Captain "Deke" Parsons, who was in charge of the explosives research, was skeptical. He said it was like "blowing in a beer can without splattering the beer." Each point of detonation on the sphere created a shock wave that interfered with all the other shock waves. They finally solved it with the study of hydrodynamics—the study of complex, dynamic fluid motions. This problem actually turned out to be a crude safety feature for some types of nuclear weapons—the one point detonation. In many future Broken Arrows, a single detonator going off would destroy the weapon without triggering a full nuclear detonation. It would scatter dangerous radiation in many cases, but prevented *the big one* from going off.

An MK-39 secondary has an estimated total weight of at least two hundred pounds, closer to three hundred, but the true amount of plutonium still in the ground at Faro is not yet known.

Richard Rhodes, a Pulitzer Prize-winning author, wrote the book *Dark Sun: The Making of the Hydrogen Bomb*. He is a nuclear historian, a type of writer that didn't exist until a few years ago. His account of Edward Teller's work in developing the thermonuclear, or second stage, is helpful in estimating the amount of plutonium that is in the secondary at Faro. Teller found that it would take a shock wave from the primary, traveling through both ends of a cylinder of deuterium, to initiate thermonuclear burning. He realized that a subcritical stick of plutonium at the center axis of the secondary would be the boost to go thermonuclear. He called that stick *the spark plug*. Using that subcritical stick as a starting point in our estimate it would stand to reason that the spark plug of a secondary would have to weigh something less than the minimum necessary for critical mass. A very early definition of critical mass, the Christy core, was 6.2 kilograms. It was a solid-core plutonium model devised by physicist Robert Christy in 1944. In 2001 the Department of Energy in its report "RDD-7" said that six kilograms of plutonium is enough, hypothetically, to make one nuclear explosive device. The subcritical portion of secondary plutonium would be less than the critical mass of six kilograms.

Plutonium is some of the nastiest stuff on earth, but some experts say that, pound for pound, it is still not "the most toxic poison known to man." That would be botulism, tetanus, and anthrax. It is still high on the lethal list. The dangers of plutonium were analyzed early in the Manhattan Project when Dr. Wright Langham, the Los Alamos expert in plutonium, did some experiments on a human body, his own, to determine how much plutonium a human could handle without danger. He actually put small quantities on his skin and drank very small quantities added to water. He determined that sixth tenths of a millionth of a gram, 0.06 microgram, was the limit the body could bear. Later the permissible *body burden* of plutonium was set at 0.65 microgram, about ten times Langham's crude estimate, but still a very small amount.

Between 1944 and 1994, the US created or acquired about 110,000 kilograms of plutonium. About one hundred thousand kilograms remain in inventory; the difference, about ten thousand kilograms, has been released, usually by atmospheric testing. Airborne, soluble chemical compounds of plutonium are considered so dangerous by the Department of Energy that the maximum permissible occupational concentration in air is an infinitesimal thirty-two trillionth of a gram per cubic meter of air. That has been compared to a grain of salt in four cubic yards of soil. Another Los Alamos expert, Dr. George Voeiz, says that no known humans have ever died from acute toxicity due to plutonium uptake, but based on animal studies the lethal dose to an average human would be twenty-two milligrams if injected, eighty-eight milligrams if inhaled. Using the benchmark of six hypothetical kilograms the plutonium in one MK-39 secondary could hypothetically equate to approximately seventy thousand deaths, but only if it was completely, absolutely, and perfectly dissipated as an aerosol, something that is certainly not likely to happen if it were underground and completely sealed inside the secondary.

Materials in the Secondary: Their Safety Hazards and Appearance

PLUTONIUM. Very lethal if inhaled, and is both a radiation hazard and a health hazard. When freshly machined, it appears similar to stainless steel, but quickly oxidizes to a dark brown or black when exposed to air. It is almost twice as heavy as lead. It is pyrophoric, which means that when exposed to air as a fine powder it is subject to spontaneous ignition. It should never be stored in water since it could explode, not as a nuclear explosion, but a chemical explosion.

URANIUM. Compared to plutonium, uranium's radioactive hazard is not as great, but the chemical toxicity is higher. If taken internally, it can cause cumulative damage to the kidneys, similar to heavy metal poisoning. When freshly machined, it appears similar to stainless steel, but oxidizes to a golden yellow color, then to black, but at a much slower rate than plutonium. Like plutonium, it is also pyrophoric as a fine powder. It is about one and a half times as heavy as lead.

LITHIUM. Is the lightest of the metals, and is a highly flammable silver-white metal, typically stored in mineral oil. It can react with water, causing tissue burns. That is why it is so dangerous to skin, which contains moisture. When cut, it shows a metallic luster that quickly turns gray, then black.

According to Sandia Labs in a report to the Air Force on another later accident investigation, the thermonuclear weapon secondary was at first thought to be "virtually indestructible." But that would be disproven by the Thule, Greenland, Broken Arrow in 1968 where impact forces shattered the bomb's secondary and the detonation of high explosives in the weapons scattered the contents. So secondaries were not "virtually indestructible" after all. The secondary at Faro could have been damaged as it broke through the nose of the weapon and penetrated the earth. But at least the conventional high explosives at Faro did not go off.

The Thule crash proved to be the straw that broke the camel's back as far as SAC's armed airborne alerts were concerned. Within twenty-four hours of the Thule Broken Arrow on January 21, 1968, the internal memo went out to: "Terminate the carrying of nuclear weapons aboard airborne alert aircraft indoctrination level missions. No publicity is being given to this fact." The *Thule Monitor* was a twenty-four-hour circling mission, primarily to guard the polar route against the Soviets and to alert SAC if a power outage occurred at the Ballistic Missile Early Warning radar station. SAC was concerned that one of the frequent ice storms could knock out communications along with the lights, and it might be interpreted as the first strike by the Soviets. So a very expensive night watchman, the *Thule Monitor*, a fully armed B-52, walked the beat twenty-four/seven over Thule to let Headquarters SAC know if they had received the first Soviet strike or if the lights had just gone out in another storm.

The Broken Arrow at **Bunker Hill** Air Force Base in Indiana on December 8, 1964, brought to light the susceptibility of the chemicals in a secondary to ignite. A B-58 Hustler, was responding to an ORI (operational readiness inspection) exercise. The sleek four-engine bomber was taxiing behind another B-58 on an icy runway to take off. It turned too close and was blown sideways off the runway by the exhaust of the airplane in front. When the landing gear went off the runway in the snow, it collapsed, and the loaded bomber caught fire. Two of the three crewmen escaped, the third ejected but was not carried high enough for his parachute to open. The aircraft had four MK-43 and one BA-53 thermonuclear weapons.

It was reported that the fire was extinguished after two hours. The following day when recovery efforts began, the secondary of one of the MK-43s burst into flames. It had been extinguished but, "when this secondary was moved, it ignited again and was extinguished with sand." It seemed the secondary had a way of self-igniting, especially when involved in violent activities like crashes.

We may understand more about what awaits us at Faro by some newly declassified information concerning the US submarine *Scorpion* sinking in 1968, and the description of the underwater debris from a nuclear torpedo: "The uranium and plutonium core of these weapons have corroded to a heavy, insoluble mass soon after the sinking and remains close to its original location inside the torpedo room. If the corroded materials were released outside the submarine, their large specific gravity and insolubility would cause them to settle in the sediment."

This complements a similar study from the Argonne National Lab EVS, where they determined that plutonium has the unique characteristic of not dissolving in water but it will attach to and *ride* on grains of sand. Typically one part of plutonium will remain in solution for every two thousand parts in sediment or soil. In wetlands it tends to settle out and adhere strongly to sediment, and will move only when the soil moves. The word sediment is a very good way to describe the deep waterlogged soil of the farmlands of Nahunta Swamp.

Dale Dusenbury, health physicist supervisor of the North Carolina Radiation Protection Service, still takes water samples from a number of shallow water wells in the Faro region. So far all samples are consistent with levels of radiation found naturally. But, he said, "The federal government has never released an accident report to us. We are not sure what is under the soil, or even if it warrants monitoring."

His water samples, however, are from wells in an area where the water table is very near the surface, not from a depth of 180 feet. In fact, the surface ground elevation of the Bomb 2 Two site is only 43 feet above the surface water level of the nearby Nahunta Swamp. That puts the buried secondary component at least 140 feet inside the water table assuming the table is the same as the swamp and level throughout the area. This underground water, known as the Northern Coastal Plain aquifer system, consists of thick sequences of porous sand beds running to and under the North Carolina coast.

Today's environmental engineers have the expertise to track toxic and dangerous chemicals from municipal waste dumps by measuring their rate of underground flow, or migration. That expertise has apparently never been put to use at Faro. An environmental engineer who reviewed this data said that any underground toxic debris at Faro, if it were fragmented, could be miles downstream after fifty years.

The Weapons Testing Context

Starting in 1951 there was a surge of nuclear testing worldwide, and the US was the leader. The following is the total number of nuclear tests worldwide for the period 1951 to 1963:

Year	Tests
1951	18
1952	11
1953	18
1954	16
1955	24
1956	33
1957	55
1958	116
1959	0
1960	3
1961	71
1962	178

(Source: Federation of American Scientists)

On August 21, 1957, something happened that affected the upward trend. President Dwight Eisenhower announced that the United States would suspend testing for two years under certain conditions. The following March the USSR announced a unilateral moratorium, provided the West would also stop testing. For two years there was a gap in the number of world nuclear tests. Between October 31, 1958, and September 14, 1961, the United States conducted no nuclear tests because of this self-imposed moratorium. The world was practically free of nuclear weapons testing. France was the only country to test in 1960 with three detonations in the Sahara Desert of Africa.

On May 1, 1960, Francis Gary Powers was shot down in his CIA U-2 spy plane over Soviet Russia.

On January 17, 1961, exactly one week before *Keep 19* crashed, and as the keynote of his farewell address as the thirty-fourth president, former five-star general Dwight Eisenhower warned of a new entity in America—the military-industrial complex: "The immense military establishment that has joined with a large arms industry is new to the American experience . . . We must not fail to comprehend its grave implications."

On September 15, 1961, the US resumed nuclear testing. On October 30, 1961, the Russians detonated the biggest thermonuclear weapon ever detonated in the world, *Tsar Bomba*. It had three stages, not two, and was designed to be one hundred megatons but was reduced to fifty megatons over the Russian's concern of world fallout. Some scientists feared that one hundred megatons would ignite the very upper atmosphere of Earth.

In 1962 Jack ReVelle traveled to Christmas Island in the South Pacific to be part of the EOD team for Operation Dominic II, a twenty-five-shot nuclear test series.

Chapter 6

The Cause of the Crash

Pushing the Design Envelope

A critical part of the development of any new aircraft is the measuring, in great detail and early on in each prototype phase, of actual flight characteristics discovered compared to the engineering expectations. This is done by plotting data points—such as weight, speed, temperature, air density, power settings, etc.—at a number of different configurations. Then in flight testing, pushing beyond those limits, in small increments and recording the responses. This is called pushing the envelope. Many who have done it also call it, "hours and hours of extreme boredom interrupted by moments of sheer terror."

Early aircraft development tended to overbuild by making the aircraft much stronger than necessary but also much safer. A good example is the DC-3, also known in the military as the C-47, a real workhorse, very difficult to overload. There was one fabled incident in the backwaters of the South Pacific where a badly damaged wing and engine of a C-47 was replaced by a much shorter fighter's wing since it was the only way of getting out of the bush. And it flew—with one engine on the good side and a much shorter wing without an engine on the other.

A better-documented example is the Lockheed C-130 Hercules, a cargo plane rated for 92 passengers or 64 airborne troops. In April 1975, a C-130 was loaded with evacuees and flown out of Saigon's Tan Son Nhut Airport. When it landed, 452 people got out, 32 of them from the flight deck.

Later the art of aircraft development would sometimes push the design *process* envelope. The G-model B-52 had a lighter weight structure than previous versions but yet it carried more fuel. It had the *wet wing*, fuel tanks which replaced the rubber-bladder types. This, combined with the elimination of the ailerons, saved weight in the wing itself and made for more internal room in the wing, which allowed for a fuel load increase of 41,000 pounds. However, the elimination of the ailerons plus relying solely on the spoilers for lateral controls along with the shorter rudder of the G-model had some rather unpleasant side effects. It increased the tendency to Dutch roll, a problem with all large, swept wing aircraft. When a pilot initiated a turn in the G-model the spoilers caused a slight buffet and the nose to pitch up, especially troubling in aerial refueling. It was exhausting for the pilots to hold it steady in the refueling position.

The B-52G wing had experienced a similar fatigue failure during cyclic testing but that was not known at the operations level—so that possibility might not have been addressed in written procedures for inspections. The wing of previous models of the B-52 had a pronounced flex limit in flight: 16 feet up and 16 feet down, a total of 32 feet. With a total wingspan of 185 feet tip to tip, the length of one wing from root to tip would be about 90 feet. That wing moving up and down over one-third of its length would have been dramatic. The G-model wing was stiffened, but still had vertical movement. Any movement would also mean the linkages inside the wing structure were moving and shifting—machinery like flaps, spoilers, and fuel and hydraulic lines. Low-level flying and the structural strains that occurred during air refueling were expected to speed up fatigue considerably. No one could forecast accurately when wing failure would happen during operations, but it was estimated that under fairly similar circumstances the operating stress placed on this new wing was approximately 60 percent higher than the stress inflicted on the wing of preceding B-52s. The problem was recognized and a $219 million wing modification was approved in May of 1961, four months after *Keep 19* crashed. The retrofit started in 1962 and was completed in 1964. The crash of *Keep 19* in January 1961 may have been the final motivation for the program. Production of the G-model ended in early 1961. The last two G-model B-52s made were delivered to the Air Force in February 1961, a month after the crash of *Keep 19*.

The relationship with Boeing and the Goldsboro crash was interesting. Major Tulloch was sure that "the experts must have decided that the wing was OK, and our only problem was the fuel leak." A call was made at 11:21 p.m. to Mr. Ed Hensley at Boeing, outlining the problem and requesting assistance. Mr. Hensley advised them to stand by but did not call back until 0015 EST, fifteen minutes after midnight—and was discussing the situation with the Command Post when *Keep 19* crashed. Boeing would take the position later that they had not completed their analysis before the Air Force made the decision to land. There was no need to land immediately, in Boeing's view, because there was plenty of fuel on board.

Today Boeing says that there probably was a failure to detect the metal fatigue crack during inspection or possibly a lack of inspection procedures. However, the Accident Review Board stated, "The aircraft records were minutely examined to determine the adequacy of aircraft maintenance. No discrepancies were found." The Air Force was backing up their crew chiefs: their guys maintained it just the way it was written up to be maintained. The Accident Report Findings also reported that the flight manual failed to point out that when a large fuel leak in a wing occurred, some structural damage was *always* associated with it, and the manual had no instructions on how to deal with it.

Item 3 of the Accident Board Findings stated:

"T.O. [Technical Order] 1B-52G-637 (ECP 951-5), requiring depot level compliance, was scheduled for 5 May 1961 during High Stress II modification. Compliance with this technical order would have prevented the failure of the #2 panel of the right wing lower skin."

Here was the classic command dilemma: a fix for a known problem was planned, but the risk of flying with it was overridden by current mission pressure. The risk of knowingly scheduling a crew to fly an aircraft with a wing defect was overridden by mission pressure in the start-up of Airborne Alerts and Chrome Dome.

It is difficult to evaluate fifty years after the accident, according to Mr. Michael Lombardi of Boeing Historical Research. He has been very helpful, and reminds us that whatever was learned from this accident has no doubt saved many lives and contributed greatly to the outstanding level of flight safety that we enjoy today.

The Weather Factor of This Crash

Officially, weather was not considered to be a factor in the crash. The mission weather portion of *AF Form 14* stated at that at 1 a.m., the time of the crash, Goldsboro weather at ten thousand feet was clear, with unlimited visibility, and winds from the west (270°), at fifty-seven knots. However, the weather dramatically deteriorated during the actual crash sequence. Consider these points:

- Three days before, the unexpected severity of a blizzard almost shut down President Kennedy's inauguration and the rebound front from this giant, circulating low-pressure area was driving into North Carolina from the west. The front itself had advanced to a position near Raleigh-Durham as of 1 a.m., the time of the crash.

- Texas Tower Four, an offshore radar dome about seventy miles east of New Jersey was completely destroyed five days before the inauguration. A "fierce winter storm" collapsed the Air Force installation with a loss of all twenty-eight men. It is not known if these storms were part of the same weather system known as the Gail of 1961. There were no weather satellites at that time.

- At the time of the crash the jet stream was "centered over Seymour Johnson AFB with winds of 160 knots at 40,000 feet; and 110 knots at 29,000 feet." Under these conditions winds at 10,000 feet would at least be considered *dynamic*.

- Within forty-eight hours after the crash, freezing rain and snow were severe enough to delay all recovery efforts. For days immediately afterward, snow and ice shut down portions of the state from Manteo to Murphy. Heavy icing stopped road traffic and cars were stranded in many areas. Goldsboro had snow for three days. On day three the high was twenty-eight degrees, and the low was ten degrees.

- Right after takeoff and during the initial climb-out, moderate to severe turbulence was experienced. Normally that would not be considered a problem, but may have been a factor in the sequence of events that followed.

- We are not sure how the winds aloft and the turbulence affected the aircraft since the VGH Gust Recorder (the *black box* of the time) was not sufficiently protected to preserve the recordings, as stated as Item 10 of the Findings. This missing information, in light of the varying wind speeds, aloft would have been extremely useful.

The Endorsement

Officer effectiveness reports (OERs) are the key to a career officer's future. This is where an Air Force officer's professional life is writ large, his permanent record. His performance factors, his over-all evaluation, and his promotion potential are all spelled out annually in excruciating detail by his immediate commander and endorsed by his boss's boss. The OER followed him around from base to base and could either be a star in his crown or an albatross to wear for the rest of his career. A bad OER could even end his career.

Scott Tulloch received *excellent* or *exceptional* ratings in all categories throughout his entire career. But the real measure of the man can be read, not in the boxes checked on the form, but in the comments section written by the reporting official. That is where you get the feel for the person. Here are some of the comments written on Major Tulloch's OERs throughout his entire career:

> Completely reliable; has mature judgment. Hard working, competent, constant smile, ready wit. Personal enthusiasm. A good family man. A most pleasing personality and his morals are beyond reproach. His greatest strength lies in his tenacious attitude. Has a keen interest in military history. Active in the community, works with the Boy Scouts. Accomplished writer. Excellent analyzer. He will not give up on a problem until it has been satisfactorily completed.

After a major aircraft accident, such as *Keep 19*, the prevailing mindset of the Air Force is to eventually set blame. With the enormous loss of equipment such as a B-52, and the potential of unfavorable public scrutiny, the unwritten rule of command structure was to find the person or persons responsible for the crash. From the OER dated July 10, 1961, the first OER written after the accident, the wing commander, Colonel Osce V. Jones, said straight out in his endorsement, "I am pleased to have him in my command." The reporting official was Lieutenant Colonel Colin Hamilton, Commander of the Seventy-Fourth Bomb Squadron, and had written in his comments: "CINCSAC, CG 8AF, and CG 822 AD stated that in effect that Major Tulloch expertly handled the emergency and that this was one of the very few aircraft accidents that crew or supervisory efforts were not in error."

CINCSAC is the Commander In Chief of the Strategic Air Command.

CG 8AF is the Commanding General of the Eighth Air Force.

CG 822 AD is the Commanding General of the 822nd Air Division.

Major Scott Tulloch had the backing and support of the brass all the way up the line from his immediate boss to commander in chief, SAC. You don't get any better backing than that.

The Worst Case

There is a frightening scenario of an accidental nuclear detonation on American soil being perceived by military leaders in 1961 not as an accident, but as a deliberate strike by the Soviets. Would cool heads wait for a confirmation that a terrible accident had just occurred, or would there be enough confusion in the fog of communications to consider it a Soviet strike? In the Cold War a B-52 bomber could be used as a show of force, it could go out there and loiter. If not needed, the aircraft could turn around and return home unused. But ICBMs were operational in 1961, and there was no fail-safe to a missile once launched. A SAC missile officer once told me, "When the missile was sitting on the pad we had control of it. One inch off the pad (at launch) and that sucker was committed all the way to the target."

If the US made such a response by accident, it would not be the first time that a country would make such a decision. The initial bombing of London in World War II was an accident. Carl Builder, an analyst for RAND wrote: "It happened on the night of August 24, 1940. Flying through the fog and clouds over England, two German bombers were separated from their radar-equipped pathfinder guiding them toward a target in the Midlands north of London. Unable to regroup, they meandered through the sky until they attracted antiaircraft fire from the ground. Knowing that they were hopelessly lost, they jettisoned their bombs and turned for home."

As things happened, the pilots were over London and the bombs did incredible damage. One bomb hit a national monument, one exploded on a church, another killed civilians coming out of a late-night movie, and more. Retaliation was nearly instant. Leonard Mosley wrote in *The Battle of Britain (World War II)*: "Churchill ordered Bomber Command to attack Berlin as a reprisal, which in turn provoked Hitler to order that London should now become his air force's main target."

The SAC bomber alert response time in 1961 of fifteen minutes was built around the time for a Soviet missile *detection to detonation* time. This is ironic, but we should remember it took about thirty to forty-five minutes for the Seymour Johnson control tower to confirm, by Mattocks' and Rardin's arrival at the main gate, that there had even been a crash. Of course had there been an actual detonation, Seymour Johnson would have witnessed it immediately from twelve miles away and may have had time to react in some way before communications were knocked out. The effect of electromagnetic pulse (EMP) on communications was not sufficiently studied until after this crash at the 1962 Starfish Prime airborne test in the mid-Pacific. That test was 1.4 megatons, and it shut off streetlights, burglar alarms, and microwave communications in Hawaii, 900 miles away. A 3.8-megaton detonation, much larger and 888 miles closer, would shut down more than burglar alarms at Seymour Johnson.

The think tanks of the 1960s were cranked up and were trying to cover every possibility of nuclear attack. One scenario had the Soviet first strike occurring inside America with smuggled nuclear devices exploding inside the Soviet Embassy in Washington, DC, and in Soviet offices near the United Nations Building in New York. A CIA officer said, "I believe there has never been a military force more difficult to surprise than SAC. SAC is a jumpy, alert-happy force. There is little if any exaggeration in saying that if small fires were to break out simultaneously in the paint lockers of three or four SAC bases in the world, the bombers of the SAC alert force (numbering in the hundreds), bombed up and fully fueled, would within approximately fifteen minutes take off and head out to their assigned targets."

If communications were so much of a problem that the wing commander had to go out to his staff car just to talk to *Keep 19*, and even if EMP did not instantly fry communications, what would be involved in convincing Washington and SAC that this had really been an accidental, not intentional, detonation? That brings up the point of the difference between a Broken Arrow, which does not create the risk of nuclear war, and a NUCFLASH, which does create the risk of nuclear war. Would an accidental detonation anywhere in the United States be falsely but intentionally designated as NUCFLASH by command and used as the excuse to finally do what so many commanders really wanted?

There are some famous quotes from that time that indicated a leaning toward preemptive nuclear strikes, even without provocation. In 1954, an overflight of the Soviet Union was planned by RB-47s from the Ninety-first Strategic Reconnaissance Wing in England with Lieutenant Colonel Hal Austin commanding. General LeMay told Austin before takeoff, "Well, maybe if we do this overflight right we can get World War III started."

It is not known if he was joking but General LeMay was not known for his humor.

General LeMay as commander in chief had already established the strategic policies of SAC in 1961. A good example of those policies was in the May 21, 1957, *top secret* remarks he made to the USAF Advisory Board at Patrick Air Force Base in Florida. He announced to the board a recent appraisal of what each Joint Chief of Staff command could actually do in the critical first hours of the *air power battle* as he called it . . . the opening first shots of World War III. Of all JCS Commands only SAC could "underwrite the destruction of 100 percent of the DGZs (designated ground zeros)," of which there were 1,539 at that time.

SAC alone	100 percent
All other JCS commands including Navy	11 percent
Navy alone	5 percent

When General LeMay left SAC in 1957 to become the vice chief of staff of the USAF, he was followed by General Thomas Power. Under General Power, SAC would not just continue the policies of LeMay, they would be hardened. Like his predecessor, General Power believed that SAC was at war. He once said, "Day and night, I have a certain percentage of my command in the air. The planes are bombed up, and they don't carry bows and arrows." General Power was commander in chief of SAC from 1957 to 1964.

When asked about restraint in the conduct of nuclear war, General Power said, "Restraint! Why are you so concerned about saving *their* lives? The whole idea is to *kill* the bastards . . . Look. At the end of the war, if there are two Americans and one Russian, we win!"

Americans had always been told that only the president, or his immediate successor, could authorize the use of nuclear weapons. In fact, instructions had been given to a number of specified air defense commanders that they could, in certain situations, use nuclear weapons on their own authority. This policy was spelled out in a document entitled *Authorization for the Expenditure of Atomic Weapons in Air Defense* and was signed by President Eisenhower. This authorization was to be used for defense only, not as an offensive measure. The authority was broadened in magnitude on May 22, 1957, by a document of *predelegation*, which listed five commanders authorized to launch a retaliatory strike if conditions made it impossible to communicate with the secretary of defense and the Joint Chiefs of Staff. Among the five commanders was CINSAC, the commander in chief of the Strategic Air Command.

John S. D. Eisenhower would write in his notes, "[The President] agreed that it is most important that word of any delegation from the President be withheld from our allies. It is in the US interest to maintain the atmosphere that all authority stays with the President without predelegation."

Not only was the document classified as top secret, the knowledge of the existence of the document would be limited to only a very few people and was denied for years by government historians. We had reached the level of *Animal House*'s "double secret probation."

The National Security Archive published the first official documents in 1998 confirming predelegation. In 2001 the archive released a second set of documents.

General Power was just as anxious to "get World War III started" as LeMay. In January 1961, when Kennedy first took office, National Security Advisor McGeorge Bundy had a meeting with the new president. This occurred around the time *Keep 19* crashed. He advised the president of the possibility that "a subordinated commander faced with a substantial Russian military action could start the thermonuclear holocaust on his own initiative if he could not reach you (by failure of communication at either end of the line)."

LeMay, in retirement, acknowledges that Power was "a sadist." Horace Wade, who was one of Power's subordinate commanders agreed: "General Power was demanding; he was mean; he was cruel, unforgiving, and he didn't have the time of day to pass with anyone. A hard, cruel individual . . . I would like to say this. I used to worry about General Power. I used to worry that General Power was not stable. I used to worry about the fact that he had control over so many weapons and weapon systems and could, under certain conditions, launch the force. Back in the days before we had real positive control [i.e., PAL locks], SAC had the power to do a lot of things, and it was in his hands, and he knew it."

There was an intriguing interview in the April 1981 issue of *Mother Jones* magazine by Gary Hanauer, when he interviewed Dr. Ralph Lapp, well-known atomic scientist and the former Executive Director of the Department of Defense's Atomic Research and Development Board.

During the interview at one point, Dr. Lapp had stated, "There were problems involved at the [Goldsboro bomb] site that I don't feel comfortable talking about."

He was asked about Ellsberg's statement that between the two bombs all six types of safety devices had failed. When asked specifically about the charges, Lapp replied to Mother Jones, "You can't get that out of me."

"Are you denying that this failure [all six types of switches] is what happened?" Hanauer asked.

"No," he said. "But you won't get anything out of me."

"Then was the problem at the site something else?"

Lapp then paused a moment and said, "I can't tell you."

The Three Graves.
Photos by author.

Francis Roger Barnish. Master Sergeant, Ninety-seventh Bomb Wing, US Air Force, World War II. Buried at Raleigh National Cemetery, 501 Quarry Road, Raleigh, North Carolina, at Section 4, Plot 130. The grave is under a huge oak tree, north of the entrance, near the main gate. The cemetery is now full, and is well maintained by the Salisbury, NC, National Cemetery. Next to Frank's grave is an unmarked grave. Records at Salisbury show that it is of his wife, June.

Decorations: Air Medal with Two Oak Leaf Clusters, Purple Heart, POW Medal, World War II Victory Medal, and the Korean Service Medal.

Eugene H. Richards. Major, 4241st Strategic Wing, US Air Force, World War II. Buried at Stephens-Memorial Gardens, 3650 Georgia Highway 17/Big A Road, Toccoa, Georgia. Fountain Section 4, Lot E-13, Space 3. Buried with wife Sue who died on January 8, 1966, five years after her husband.

Decorations: Air Medal With Seven Oak Leaf Clusters, World War II Victory Medal.

Eugene Shelton. Major, 4241st Strategic Wing, US Air Force, World War II. Buried at Fort Sam Houston National Cemetery, 1520 Harry Wurzbach Road, San Antonio, Texas. Section H, Plot 355-A. Next to him is an unmarked grave. He had enlisted at Fort Sam Houston at age twenty-two.

Decorations: Air Force Commendation Medal.

PART II

Chapter 7

After Goldsboro

Aftermath

The Goldsboro accident happened during the decade when we were starting to look hard at all things nuclear. We improved the safety devices on our bombs and began to seriously explore nuclear energy for peace. Just four years before the crash of *Keep 19*, the first nuclear power plant opened at Shippingport, Pennsylvania, operated solely for peaceful use. We were delighted—we thought we had invented something new, but we really only discovered it. It had been there all along since the dawn of creation. After all, the sun is a continuous chain of nuclear explosions, which makes our attempts to mimic it seem puny. We were in a new era. We thought we had the answers to our increasing need for energy. In his book *Future Shock*, Alvin Toffler stated that most of the energy ever expended on Earth has been created and used in just one lifetime: ours.

Nationally, we were at the top of our game; we were scared but knew we had the ability to retaliate against our primary foe, the Soviets, if such a need arose. After all, we had SAC and LeMay. Curtis LeMay had nothing to do with the Manhattan Project team in the 1940s, but he was just the right man to take what they had built and use it to create the behemoth that became SAC in the 1960s.

In Part II, I would like to share some of my thoughts on what it was like in the Strategic Air Command after 1961, and some of the things we have learned since then, and what we still have to deal with—things and places like Chernobyl and Fukushima. We should be grateful that Goldsboro is not connected with these two names.

This Broken Arrow was central to the continued improvement of safety devices that increased dependability to a new level. It helped further refine the systems of PALs (permissive action links), to prevent a weapon from arming itself without external action. Two examples of PALs on the G-model are the pilot's readiness switch and the EW's manual cable lock handle, both required an external action. This is known as a strong link—a mechanical device that must be properly activated. The same thing applied to the ARM/SAFE switch, which was controlled by the radar navigator. A strong link isolates a weapon's firing set and detonators from all electrical signals. A weak link is designed to fail during a fire or accident before the strong link can be utilized. One example of a weak link is a Mylar capacitor in a weapon fire set. If the weapon experienced an excessively high temperature, such as in a fuel fire, the Mylar would melt and prevent the weapon firing system from going to the detonators. A weak link would be any of the other devices that would *fail to dud*. In other words, a failure of this device would not allow a subsequent action to occur.

Many of the safety procedures were the brainchild of Dr. John Foster, a physicist of the Livermore Corporation, in cooperation with Sandia Laboratories and Western Electric. In 1962 after the Goldsboro incident, such procedures designed by Dr. Foster were adopted into the US nuclear arsenal and later NATO.

There would be many other generations of strong-link/weak-link modifications following Goldsboro, all to help strengthen the potential weaknesses of the ARM/SAFE switch as pointed out in the 1998 Sandia Report. Concepts for improved nuclear safety created such things as *direct optical initiation* and *paste extrudable explosives*. These are wonders of science, keys to Thor's Hammer, tiny, some as small as a quarter.

Regardless of all safety policy procedures, the joint authority for national nuclear activity, the Atomic Energy Commission and the Department of Defense, made clear the reality: "Nuclear weapons are designed with great care to explode only when deliberately armed and fired. Nevertheless, there is always a possibility that, as a result of accidental circumstances, an explosion will take place inadvertently. Although all conceivable precautions are taken to prevent them, such accidents might occur in areas where weapons are assembled and stored, during the course of loading and transportation on the ground, or when actually in the delivery vehicle, e.g., an airplane or a missile." (AEC/DOD, *The Effects of Nuclear Weapons, 1962*).

Robert McNamara said, "We all make mistakes. There *is* a learning period—but there isn't going to be a learning period in nuclear weapons. You make *one mistake*, nations are going to be destroyed."

Two Examples of Mistakes

October 25, 1962. Volk Field, Wisconsin. Not a Broken Arrow, but an interesting event—a cautionary tale of the times during the Cuban Missile Crisis as reported by Michael Dobbs in his book, *One Minute To Midnight*. Nuclear-armed F-101s and F-106s had been dispersed to civilian airfields all over the country in a plan to avoid destruction by Russian or Cuban missiles. Some of the airfields were used mainly as auxiliary training landing strips, and were not operational airports. At Volk Field, Wisconsin, there was no hangar for the alert planes, no ILS, no Klaxon, and no control tower. At one airport in California, Siskiyou County Airport, there was "virtually nothing except a runway and a converted dental van that served as a control tower." At Duluth, Minnesota, a guard fired at an intruder coming over the fence, triggering alarms to go off all over the network. At Volk Field, pilots raced to the planes, each armed with a MB-1 Genie nuclear-tipped missile. The assumption was that they would head north to intercept the Soviet Bears and Bisons believed to be swarming over the pole. Lieutenant Dan Barry was pulling onto the runway in a snowstorm when a Jeep with lights flashing kept coming down the runway straight at his aircraft. A message had come in from Duluth canceling the alert. Since there was no control tower at Volks, the only way to stop the jet was by physically blocking the runway. Back at Duluth guards eventually concluded the fence-climbing intruder was a bear.

June 3 and 6, 1980. A NORAD computer at Colorado Springs, Colorado, registered an alarm indicating a massive Soviet missile attack. One hundred nuclear-armed B-52s were alerted for immediate takeoff. The mistake was caught and the bombers stood down. Three days later the same identical warning was given. Again one hundred SAC bombers were alerted. The problem was traced to an integrated circuit in a computer, which was producing random digits that were reflected as missiles launched. This is reminiscent of the October 5, 1960, incident at Thule. NORAD received a massive Soviet ICBM strike approaching the United States. A computer fault removed two zeros in the radar ranging components and was picking up radar returns from the surface of the moon, which was rising for the first time after the system was activated in a certain configuration.

At its inception SAC had an original response time based solely on World War II experience: six hours. They would assemble the crew, fuel the bomber, get the bomb from storage, load it, and take off. The goal was to speed things up wherever possible. The six-hour ground alert was soon reduced to one hour for one-third of the armed and ready bomber fleet to be off the ground. When it was anticipated that the Soviets would have an operational ICBM with a detection-to-detonation time of fifteen minutes, this became SAC's goal: launch of bombers in fifteen minutes. That was the reason for the fifteen-minute ground alert.

Response was measured by two exercises: *Bravo*, where the crews raced to the aircraft and started engines, and *Coco*, where they started engines and taxied to the takeoff position. There were times when SAC went to a higher intensity DEFCON, or defense condition, and the twenty-four-hour airborne alert was born, in which a classified percentage of bombers, tankers, and flying command posts were in the air at all times. It would continue until January 29, 1968. Under the twenty-four-hour airborne alert policy, if a mission had to be cut short for any reason another aircraft would immediately launch to fill the slot, which, in turn, would either move up another mission behind it or stretch out current missions. Every SAC crewmember was very aware of the intense pressure to continue every single mission regardless of problems that turned up in flight, some of which continued into accidents.

A good example of mission pressure occurred just seven weeks after the Goldsboro crash when a B-52, flying out of Mather Air Force Base, California, had a series of problems beginning with uncontrollable cabin heat and ending with a crash. While suffering for hours and hours of unstoppable and unbearable 160°F heat in the cockpit, the crew attempted to cool the airplane by depressurizing it in order to continue the mission. Then they had to go to a lower altitude to recover two crewmembers who had gotten *the bends*. Glass in instruments and windows began to crack from the heat. At times, there was only one pilot on the top deck, trying to give the others relief. After twenty grueling hours, mental miscalculations of fuel use at the lower altitude began to mount up, but still they were making every effort to continue the mission. When the low-fuel situation was finally recognized, a rescue launch of a refueling tanker aircraft was quickly made in an attempt to meet the low-flying bomber and save it, but the B-52 actually ran out of fuel within sight of the tanker, and crashed near Yuba City. Unlike *Keep 19* all eight crewmembers successfully bailed out, and the two thermonuclear bombs on board were safely recovered.

There were also communication problems at Goldsboro. Lieutenant Wilson, EW officer, tried repeatedly to use the normal high frequency radio on various channels, but it failed. Seymour Johnson also had communications problems. Command Post radios were sometimes unable to make contact with the aircraft, so about half the time the wing commander was outside in the Command Post parking lot using the more reliable radio in his staff car. Also, this was a long in-flight emergency and the tape recorder in the Command Post was frequently turned off to save tape and was not always turned back on before radio transmissions were started.

Jim Oskins and Mike Maggelet are two retired former Air Force specialists who between them have over thirty-five years of experience working in nuclear weapons technology. They have completed their second book on Broken Arrows. (*Broken Arrow Volume II, A Disclosure of Significant U.S., Soviet, and British Nuclear Weapon Accidents and Accidents, 1945-2008*). In their first book they set the number of US Broken Arrows at thirty-six, the number announced by the Department of Defense in 1980. Now they are raising the total to sixty based on recently declassified materials and indicate there may be more, but the declassification process could run well beyond the year 2012. They point out that they have never encountered any efforts by any government agency to cover up or hinder their research. The main problem they ran into was the poor conditions of the historical records, and there is no single agency source for requests under the Freedom of Information Act. They also point out that there has never been even a partial, inadvertent US nuclear detonation reported. All detonations involved conventional high explosives only. Everything they report has been declassified.

They found an interesting document entitled, *Jettisoning Of Nuclear Weapons from DOD Aircraft*, which outlines procedures on how to handle press statements to the general public. "If the (jettisoned) weapon lands in circumstances such as to be publicly unobserved, no statement should be indicated." In other words, if nobody in the civilian world saw it, it would not be reported to the press.

After *Keep 19* many details surrounding the crash at Goldsboro remained hidden for years behind the cloak of secrecy in accordance with Department Of Defense policy. Now, fifty years later, important records are being declassified. Although normal DOD policy is to neither confirm nor deny the presence of nuclear weapons, recently revised DOD Directive 5230.16, which governs public affairs, allows for confirmation when it is deemed necessary for public safety or it is needed to reduce widespread public alarm. *The Accident Report* itself, (*AF Form 14* including *Findings*) has now been declassified and located, as well as the crew's *History Of Flight*, along with the 1998 study by Sandia Corporation entitled *The History of Nuclear Safety Devices. The Explosive Ordnance Disposal Report*, written by First Lieutenant Jack ReVelle, EOD team commander has been discovered. Internal letters with reports from the Atomic Energy Commission are now available. Of course, some words and phrases are still redacted, or blacked out, but by using the details now available plus other reliable sources there are three things now apparent: the collapse of the right wing was caused by the massive fuel loss caused by a design failure; at least to some degree we came close to nuclear disaster; and there is still some dangerous stuff at Faro.

The Lady with the Microphone

In 2011 Adam Mattocks said about the crash: "I feel bad about the crash, the crew did everything they could to save the plane and to protect the community. It was our mission to be ready to deliver that weapon onto the target, wherever that target might be—and to get out of there fast. If we got out, we knew we probably not survive getting back into our own country, for our own country would be so much on the defensive that we would probably get shot down by our own people, that is, even if we got out of Russia. All of the targets were deep inside Russia and we would have a lot of mainland to go over, a long way to go to get out. We knew we would have to go to a neutral country, and either land there or bail out there if we ran out of fuel."

He was standing out in a field next to Big Daddy's Road at the site of the crash a half a century after it all happened. It was a bright, chilly day, a lot like that day in 1961, and it was very windy. A cold front was coming through just like then. A pretty lady was interviewing him with a microphone in her hand, a television cameraman behind her, recording Adam for the night's news. We were standing with Dr. Jack ReVelle, who had carried the core of an atomic bomb in his hands up a ladder at that very spot in that field. Shortly before, Jack and I were hunkered over a GPS receiver, finding a coordinate. This was the spot. We looked up and saw a caravan of cars, SUVs, and TV satellite trucks pulling off the road on to the dirt lane where we were. "What is this, the *Field Of Dreams?*" asked Jack. The vehicles were strung out along the dirt road in the field.

I was watching the lady with the microphone as she asked Adam and Jack the important questions, thinking ahead, guiding the interview to cover all the important points. She was so caught up in the story that she began to lose focus a little bit. And at some point, just for a few minutes, she stopped being the reporter; she became someone who was fascinated by what she heard, just listening to the real history of that place told by two men who had never met before, and who had not been back there in fifty years. The cameraman behind her asked Adam a question, not to get the interview back on track but because he, the cameraman, wanted to hear more about the details of the place where he was standing. He, too, was caught up in the history. Adam paused, gathering his thoughts. He spoke in careful, measured words. He looked away to the west, toward the sun, like he was trying to peer through the mists of time. He turned around as if to fix himself at the correct spot on Earth. Maybe he was remembering his prayers of that night, and measuring himself against those promises made. Something was going on here.

"Every member of that crew should be honored in some way. Some gave their lives . . ."

Adam Mattocks, last surviving member of Keep 19, giving an onsite TV interview on the fiftieth anniversary of the crash. Photo by author

Fifty years ago both of these men arrived at that same spot, a few hours apart, both by jet aircraft: Adam Mattocks by jumping out of a disintegrating B-52, Jack ReVelle by a T-33, a special delivery from Wright-Patterson Air Force Base.

Crash Prevention

We also have to ask the question: could some sort of crew intervention have prevented the crash of *Keep 19*? The short answer is no. There was no way that the crew of *Keep 19* could have kept the wing on that aircraft. It was a crash waiting to happen, if not with that crew, with some other aircrew. The fact that they did not know of the extensive damage to the lateral controls kept them from making different decisions early on that could have possibly limited loss of life. The experts had told them from the ground that the only problem they had was the fuel leak and that was already resolved. The crew knew that Boeing had been contacted, but they didn't know that Boeing had not yet called back with helpful information.

If the crew could somehow have known everything, they might have lightened up the airplane by using up even more fuel and gone for a no-flaps landing. But even that is a huge gamble with two engines out, the possibility of fire, and the risk of leaking fuel. They didn't know if the flaps would work at all, that's why the Command Post wanted a flaps test at a higher altitude. When they started the flaps test, Approach Control had them begin the intercepting turn to the airport.

Another B-52 pilot said, "If you had a choice, and could get the guys on the bottom out, and if things turned to [bad word] during the approach, better to have only the guys with the upwards seats." Major Tulloch said that he wanted to bail out everyone but himself and the copilot, but he needed the navigators to guide them around populated areas in the dark. There was no way for the extras to bail out without the navigator ejecting. Actually, there was one other extremely remote possibility: the aft equipment compartment hatch, but it was way back in the tail, a difficult distance on the other side of the unpressurized wheel wells and both bomb bays. It was for the use of ground crews to access equipment in the tail and not a realistic possibility of escape for a flight crew in an emergency.

Major Tulloch said, "I'd flown many a bombing raid at night and those folks sleeping down there [in North Carolina] were depending on us to defend them, not rain flaming death and destruction on them in the middle of the night."

To quote a former pilot, when pressed for some Monday morning quarterbacking: "So without knowing what transpired with the guys on the ground and the discussions with Boeing, I would hesitate to second-guess the guys on the sharp end. I just can't judge the guy in charge. But there was no way he could have prevented that crash."

The Danger Today

There are three apparent dangers at Faro today:
The biggest danger is the presence of any toxic materials from the secondary in the ground between 72 and 180 feet down, just north of the

old cemetery on Big Daddy's Road. The 72-foot depth was based on the EOD's maximum 50-foot probe of the hole of travel of the secondary, which was done from the 22-foot level of the dig. The 180-foot depth, plus or minus 10 feet, was based on the University of North Carolina study. Although the exact depth is not known, the geographical location of that danger from the secondary is known: it is beneath the center of the 400-foot circle easement. That is unless fragmented materials have migrated downstream in the aquifer. See BOMB LOCATIONS in the attached Appendix F.

The second greatest danger is any souvenir .50 caliber bullet sitting in someone's closet. Fifty caliber bullets are very powerful and these would be either incendiary, explosive, or armor piercing, designed to shoot down enemy aircraft and missiles. If any were still around today, fifty years later, they would be very unstable and extremely dangerous. If someone banged one around it could go off and either burn their house down, blow their house up, or shoot through their house. It would be a supreme tragedy if the only Faro casualty from the Goldsboro Broken Arrow was the death or injury of someone's grandchild, or great-grandchild, years after the crash of *Keep 19*. The chief of the Faro Fire Department agreed to handle any reported shells with the explosive ordnance disposal flight commander at Seymour Johnson Air Force Base. That announcement has been made at every event where the author speaks about the Goldsboro Broken Arrow. There were about twenty-four hundred bullets in the four tail guns of *Keep 19*. We do not know how many shells have been recovered and turned in.

The third potential danger could be whatever is in those fifty-five-gallon metal drums buried in a deep hole north of bomb site two. They probably contain oil- or fuel-soaked dirt. Protection of the environment was not an important issue in the 1960s, like it is today. That location is unknown, but it is somewhere north of the cemetery on Big Daddy's Road.

In a report by the Los Alamos Laboratory, which was obtained in 2004, the protocol for making the Faro site *safe* concluded: "After the aircraft debris was removed, the bomb crater was filled, the impact area was purchased, a concrete slab poured over the area, the area fenced, and notices posted prohibiting digging."

As Scott Hardy said in his thesis, "All the measures seem reasonable and responsible to secure the site. Sadly, in the above statement, 'The bomb crater was filled' seems to be the only true portion. The others, based on testimony of witnesses and the landowner, are falsehoods. It appears the area was never purchased, never had a concrete slab poured over the top, had never been fenced in, and the only signs that have been put in the area have been posted for the purpose of hunting."

"The question must be asked," Hardy continued, "Why would the United States Government produce a classified document for the use of scientists at Los Alamos that contains obvious fabrications of procedures to insure the public safety? The only rational conclusion is that the statements in the document are what should have been done to secure the site. But it appears the only procedures ever initiated by the government were those in the statement on the easement agreed to by Charles Davis. When Mr. Davis read the document, he laughed and said, 'None of this is true.' Sadly, Davis is right. The site is clearly visible from the road. None of the measurements laid out in the Los Alamos document seem to have ever been implemented."

The Costs

The cost of locating and recovering the secondary at Faro was quoted at the time to be $500,000 in 1961. Today that would equal around $3.6 billion. The plutonium is probably still contained within the metal cylinder—that is, if it was not damaged on impact or during its travel down through the soft, wet earth of the Nahunta Swamp. There was no trace of radiation down to as far as they could dig, around 45 feet, so it was probably OK that far. But we don't know what happened from that point on down. The long-term danger of just leaving it alone is a question yet to be answered.

We should keep Faro in mind as we watch how the world wrestles with two new ongoing nuclear accidents. We should also count the costs of those accidents as they add up.

The $3.6 billion cost of recovery from the Faro nuclear accident is minuscule compared to two others—the 2011 Japanese disaster and the 1986 Chernobyl disaster. There was horrible radiation poisoning at both sites, none at Goldsboro. At Chernobyl, a new two billion dollar shield is now being planned for the Russian reactor, to replace the crumbling steel and concrete sarcophagus currently surrounding it. When the sarcophagus was built in the 1990s it was thought that it could contain escaping radiation from the reactor fire. It was designed "like a house of cards," said Eric Schmieman of the Battele Memorial Institute. It was just pieces of metal leaning against one another and hooked together. "There are no welded joints or bolted joints—it wouldn't take much of a seismic event to knock it down." But we have found that radiation does unusual things to steel and concrete, and we don't have a lot of experience in measuring radiation effects on huge masses of building materials. That falls under the category of "things we are now learning the hard way."

The new containment device will be a half-dome built on rails beside the wreckage and then rolled over it. When it is finished the shield will be the largest movable structure in the world, taller than the Statue of Liberty at its highest point, and it will weigh twenty thousand tons. Supposedly it was designed to last for one hundred years, hopefully long enough for workers to get inside to dismantle the reactor site. It will also have three remotely controlled cranes inside to assist. So far the Russians have agreed to pay only 1 percent of the cost. They say it happened in the Ukraine, which is now no longer part of Russia. The project remains unfunded. European Union nations have promised to pay for half the cost.

When Chernobyl happened it was reported as the worst nuclear disaster in history, a Level Seven on the International Nuclear Event Scale. Japanese officials now say the Fukushima disaster has skipped from Level Five (Accident with Wider Consequences), right over Level Six (Serious), straight to Level Seven, a Major Accident. Now there are two Level Seven nuclear accidents, Chernobyl and Fukushima. The 300 mile long, 150 mile wide floating island of wreckage washed away from Fukushima will probably reach Hawaii in 2012, and California in 2014. The effects of the radioactive cooling water that was drained into the sea is unknown.

The costs of Chernobyl so far are:

18 billion rubles, about 12 billion US dollars

350,000 people relocated

500,000 workers involved in the cleanup

31 deaths of emergency workers at the time, could reach 4,000

985,000 deaths, as estimated by Russian publication, *Chernobyl*, between 1986-2004

The costs of Fukushima were: 13,000 dead, with 13,000 missing. Other costs: yet to be determined.

Goldsboro compares to these two nuclear accidents only in *potential* destruction. But what is comparable are the root causes. All three accidents began with the idea that we knew just about everything there was to know about consequences. In reality we are pretty pompous creatures. We tended to have a great deal of faith in ourselves in the fields of nuclear physics, aeronautics, natural, and other sciences. What we did not have, at least in the 1950s and 1960s, was a lot of experience in combining possible future anomalies and in estimating the results of those combinations.

Before man first walked on the moon a lot of people thought there was a good chance of that event happening. They didn't know *how* or *when* it would happen but they could visualize it years before it actually occurred. People also had a good idea that television was going to be invented years before it actually was. What few people could grasp, right up to shortly before it occurred, was the idea that billions of people on earth would be able to see the first man walk on the moon via television. It was the connection of the two different concepts that was the surprise, relatively speaking.

To reduce the causes of these three accidents down to the base points:

Chernobyl happened because of a combination of poor reactor design plus a decision to run a test with inexperienced people and incorrectly calibrated Geiger counters. Then another power plant on the circuit unexpectedly shut down, which threw additional electrical demand onto Chernobyl. The crew did not know of the developing danger when the second unexpected power surge started the chain of events. The chain of *causes* was relatively slow and unimpressive, but the conclusion was fast and dramatic.

Fukushima Daiichi happened because of a poorly designed reactor placed in the wrong location, combined with lax government oversight. The electrical generating plant, powered by nuclear energy, was built in the 1960s using the latest engineering and scientific methods. It was designed to withstand a 7.9 magnitude earthquake, bigger than practically anyone could possibly imagine at that time. The unexpected 9.0 earthquake was ten times bigger than 7.9, and it caused a ten-meter tsunami to wash over a six-meter seawall and flood the pumps, which started the chain of events. Again, the chain of *causes* was relatively slow, beginning with the design and placement, but the conclusion was fast and dramatic when another element was added, the earthquake/tsunami combo.

The Goldsboro Broken Arrow happened because a wing was poorly designed to offset a need for more fuel capacity. Then a fuel leak caused more pressure on a cracked wing panel than it could stand. The unexpected wing collapse happened so fast that not all crewmembers could react quickly enough. Again: slow chain of causes, fast chain of events.

This comparison is admittedly extremely simplistic, not intended to deprecate any event, but to point out that modern disasters usually do not have one main cause; they have multiple causes. Usually, each cause is not beyond the realm of possibility in itself but combined with other unexpected events can be very surprising and unpredictable. Combined with the compression of time and the level of seriousness, results can be catastrophic, and the costs can continue to accumulate for a long time.

The Far Future

"Six weeks ago, when I first heard about the reactor damage at the Fukushima Daiichi plant in Japan, I knew the prognosis: if any of the containment vessels or fuel pools exploded, it would mean millions of new cases of cancer in the Northern Hemisphere." So said Dr. Helen Caldicott, a prominent physician known worldwide as a cofounder of Physicians for Social Responsibility. She says that we are decades away from seeing the full effects from the radioactive emissions from Chernobyl in 1986, and it will be the same for Fukushima. That wasn't the stance of some commentators who asserted that there were relatively few genetic abnormalities in survivors' offspring.

"This is dangerously ill-informed and shortsighted; if anyone knows better, it's doctors like me. There's great debate about the number of fatalities following Chernobyl; the International Atomic Energy Agency has predicted that there will be only about four thousand deaths from cancer, but a 2009 report published by the New York Academy of Sciences says that almost one million people have already perished from cancer and other diseases. The high dose of radiation caused so many miscarriages that we will never know the number of genetically damaged fetuses that did not come to term. And both Belarus and Ukraine have group homes full of deformed children.

"As we know from Hiroshima and Nagasaki, it takes years to get cancer. Leukemia takes only five to ten years to emerge, but solid cancers take fifteen to sixty. Furthermore, most radiation-induced mutations are recessive; it can take many generations for two recessive genes to combine to form a child with a particular disease, like my specialty, cystic fibrosis. We can't possibly imagine how many cancers and other diseases will be caused in the far future by the radioactive isotopes emitted by Chernobyl and Fukushima."

Dr. Caldicott is in a controlled fury. She is furious, among other things, because radiation is so slow—if it were much faster everyone could see more easily the dangers it holds. She says doctors must do more than just treat cancer, they must enter the nuclear debate. Doctors know that there is no such thing as a safe dose of radiation, that radiation is cumulative, and that we all carry several hundred genes for disease. There are now more than twenty-six hundred genetic diseases on record and any one of which may be caused by radiation-induced mutation. At the beginning we had no sense about radiation-induced cancer. Marie Curie and her daughter didn't know that the radioactive materials they handled would kill them. But it didn't take long for the early nuclear physicists, like Dr. Wright Langham in the Manhattan Project, to recognize the toxicity of radioactive elements. Dr. Caldicott knew many of those physicists well; she says physicists had the knowledge to begin the nuclear age, and that physicians have the knowledge, credibility, and legitimacy to end it.

She is also very explicit in describing the power that lobbyists have in the US Congress in giving attention to those in her own profession: "For many years now, physicists employed by the nuclear industry have been outperforming doctors, at least in politics and the news media. Since the Manhattan Project in the 1940s, physicians have had easy access to Congress. They had harnessed the energy inside the center of the sun, and later physicists, whether lobbying for nuclear weapons or nuclear energy, had the same power. They walk into Congress and Congress virtually prostrates itself. Their technological advancements are there for all to see: the harm will become apparent only decades later.

"Doctors, by contrast, have fewer dates with Congress, and much less access on nuclear issues. We don't typically go around discussing the latent period of carcinogenesis and the amazing advances made in understanding radiology. But as a result, we do an inadequate job of explaining the long-term dangers of radiation to policymakers and the public."

Pipe Cleaning

In the fall of 2007, workers at the Byron nuclear power plant in Illinois were using a wire brush to clean a badly corroded steel pipe—one in a series that circulate cooling water to essential emergency equipment—when something unexpected happened: the brush poked through. The resulting leak caused a twelve-day shutdown of the two reactors for repairs. The plant's owner, the Exelon Corporation had long known that corrosion was thinning most of the pipes. But rather than fix them, it repeatedly lowered the minimum thickness it deemed safe. By the time the pipe broke, Exelon had declared that pipe walls just three-hundredths of an inch thick—less than one-tenth the original minimum thickness—would be good enough . . . No documented inspections of the pipes was made by anyone from the NRC for at least the last eight years preceding the leak, and the agency also failed to notice that Exelon kept lowering the acceptable standard.

The New York Times, Sunday, May 8, 2011

Tornado

On April 29, 2011, the worst tornado outbreak in forty years ripped through seven southern states killing over 360 people. Tuscaloosa, Alabama, "looks like Hiroshima" after a mile-wide tornado struck that town. TVA's Browns Ferry nuclear plant thirty miles west of Huntsville went off-line due to the storm. Emergency generators kept the water pumps going, keeping the reactor cores covered.

Browns Ferry also happens to be the source of the worst, but not widely reported, nuclear accident in America, at least until Three Mile Island occurred four years later. On March 22, 1975, two electricians at the Browns Ferry plant were down under the control room checking for air leaks in the wiring tunnel that ran between reactors. They were using strips of spongy material to seal the leaks, at arm's length in a wiring chase, a tight utility tunnel. They were testing for airflow from the leaks by using a lighted candle and watching the direction of the flame. The material they were using to fill the cracks was extremely flammable polyurethane foam.

The insulation sparked when a gust pulled the candle flame into a gap in the wiring chase. A major fire resulted and a combination of events almost led to a nuclear core meltdown. The fire severed control, communications, and the telemetry and data links between the control room and the reactor core. Other problems were soon discovered: the plant's emergency phone numbers were incorrect, fire control devices were somehow sealed off and not available, air breathing units were unusable, fire hose connections were mismatched. When the control room lost the entire electrical system, warning systems became inoperative and the water level in the core dropped from two hundred inches to a dangerous forty-eight inches. The fire burned out of control for six hours while makeshift pumping somehow kept the fuel rods covered enough. "Meltdown was averted by a thin margin."

Ironically, it was discovered that just two days before, a similar fire had started the exact same way but had been extinguished successfully. After the first fire, the shift engineers and assistant shift engineers met. According to one of them, "We discussed among the group the procedures for using lighted candles for checking for air leaks. Our conclusion was that the procedure should be stopped."

Except for one news release written March 27, 1975, the Nuclear Regulatory Commission in Washington, DC, has remained silent about Browns Ferry. The cost of correcting the design flaw of wiring tunnels for all reactors was estimated to be between seven and twelve billion dollars.

It took thirty years for the Nuclear Regulatory Commission to get effective fireproofing installed in nuclear reactors. During those thirty years, according to two internal agency investigations, the NRC approved a whole string of ineffective fire barrier materials. Even after the materials were installed in dozens of plants, the materials did not work as advertised. One of those materials was a product called Thermo-Lag, which the commission approved on what was later determined to be fraudulent lab tests submitted by an obscure company. "No inspector ever checked out the lab or to question the results," said George Mulley, a former investigator with the Inspector General's office. "There were good fire barrier materials on the market from 3M and other companies that people knew and trusted," he said. "But these plant operators kept complaining that they were too expensive. So some company that no one has ever heard of comes along, with tests from a lab that no one has ever heard of, for a material that's cheaper than anything else on the market, and the NRC says, 'Perfect! Use this!'"

Critics of the NRC say the agency's failures are especially disturbing because the very creation of the agency by Congress in the 1970s was to separate the government's roles as safety regulator and promoter of nuclear energy—an inherent conflict of interest. The same conflict that was present under its predecessor the Atomic Energy Commission.

"It wasn't much of a change," said Peter Bradford, a former NRC commissioner who now teaches at Vermont Law School. "The NRC inherited the regulatory staff and adopted the rules and regulations of the AEC intact."

In 1985 the Tennessee Valley Authority shut down all of its reactors because of a variety of safety problems that industry experts say mostly boiled down to bad management. The others reopened, but Browns Ferry Unit One stayed closed for twenty-two years.

The NRC finally declared the fire barrier Thermo-Lag "inoperable" in 1992 after independent fire tests revealed that the barrier was as combustible as "treated plywood," and required utilities to have hourly fire patrols. But it has not ordered the inoperable fire barriers to be removed and replaced.

This attitude of the overseer of the nuclear reactor business also brought the Davis-Besse nuclear plant in Ohio to the brink, again, to the worst American nuclear accident *since* Three Mile Island. On August 3, 2001, the commission asked twelve nuclear plants to conduct inspections of the control nozzles that penetrate the vessel heads at most reactors. The commission had evidence of potentially dangerous cracks and leaks in those nozzles. The agreement was to wait until the end of the calendar year to comply. FirstEnergy Corp., owner of Davis-Besse, said it would comply, but not until March 22 of the following year. In the test of wills that followed, it was the NRC that blinked. On March 6 workers started on the inspection and found that acid in the cooling water had eaten almost completely through the lid of the reactor. The plant then closed for two years for emergency repairs, two FirstEnergy engineers were convicted for lying to investigators and the company paid more than $33.5 million in civil and criminal penalties.

"They should have just shut them down," said George Mulley, who investigated the case. "But the attitude at NRC was always, 'You can't shut them down, they'll fight us in court!'"

A Cup of Coffee (My Opinion)

We are more than lucky that we are not comparing Goldsboro with Chernobyl and Fukushima today, that we are not having a National Fiftieth Anniversary Memorial of a tragedy. Goldsboro was not "the worst man-made catastrophe in the world" as feared by the International Peace Institute, mainly because the ARM/SAFE switch worked. But it was 100 percent fatal to three airmen and their families.

We are now at a place in history where we can look back with the accumulated knowledge from a half a century and with access to previously classified documents now available under the Freedom of Information Act. With those documents along with the benefit of personal accounts and the analyses of others, we can gain insight into what this crew faced during this time of peril in 1961. This was a tragic aircraft accident with the loss of three brave, professional airmen. It could have been so much worse: a nuclear explosion on American soil, hundreds of times bigger than Hiroshima.

This crew, flying a heavy aircraft with a known structural design weakness, fighting the sluggish spoiler controls during exhausting refuelings, and after three hours of crisis, faced a chain of progressive problems that was unknowingly still growing. During a night approach to landing, while slowing from 220 to 180 knots, the aircraft made a sixty-degree turn to the left into freshly gusting headwinds, with landing gear already down, two engines out on the right side, and going to full flaps. This condition is known to pilots as a *dirty airplane*—not aerodynamically clean. These elements would never have been even remote factors, certainly not enough to pull the wing off a B-52. It is now apparent that during the flap extension something reached the breaking point in the wing, perhaps in the vicinity of the hydraulic lines controlling the right spoilers. Maybe a ruptured hydraulic line caused one or more of the control panels to activate, which created drag and the turn to the right. The pilots ran out of airspeed and control at the same time. Obviously, this aircraft had more compounding stresses on a damaged wing than it could abide: structural damage to the right wing combined with an attempt to stop a barrel roll to the right with only two engines on the far right side was too much.

It began earlier with the small fatigue crack in a wing skin, which led to the huge loss of fuel, which in turn led to internal structural damage to the right wing controls—damage that was not known until the flaps were lowered. When the control surfaces jammed, the airplane continued the turn until it rolled, the right wing cracked, folded upward, and the big aircraft came apart.

We constantly worry about nuclear materials in the hands of terrorists but we have forgotten about some dangerous dust in the back of our own closet: the secondary buried at Faro. Our descendants are going to have to clean it up someday. Perhaps they will have both the tools and the desire to do so, if only someone will remember where we put it. That's one of the reasons to write this stuff down.

Few people thought about terrorists in 1961, but Adam Mattocks later said the crew realized if they had to bail out over the ocean at least they would let the aircraft go down and be in water deep enough so no enemy would find the bombs.

Maybe that was the thinking of the Air Force in leaving the secondary alone. Maybe they thought that 180 feet down in the wet earth at Faro was just as impossible to retrieve as a nuclear weapon in deep ocean water. But today, bridge and tunnel builders go to far greater depths. We can cap an oil well a mile underwater, and pluck Chilean miners from a depth twelve times the depth of the secondary at Faro.

We have a distinct advantage in analyzing the thought process of the nuclear weapons scientists and engineers of the time of *Keep 19*. Being able to read their own words, written over a period of decades, is a unique window into the minds and souls of those patriotic Americans who so desperately wanted to protect their homeland. They did their absolute best to achieve these national goals, and it is interesting to witness from afar their worries, doubts, and concerns about working through the quest to create the perfect weapon—never before seen on Earth—that at the same time could be a horrible monster of unknown capabilities that might devour us all in our beds. Hopefully, we can learn from those events of 1961 and the current events we read about today.

The crisis in Japan continues at the time this is written. Hopefully it will not reach the China syndrome stage as named by Dr. Lapp. Instead of theoretically melting through the core of the earth all the way to China, since China is right next door to Japan it would theoretically melt all the way through the earth to somewhere off the east coast of South America. We may call it the Brazil syndrome.

In both incidents (Goldsboro and Japan) the best and brightest minds of the 1950s and 1960s created a newer version of two old items (a weapon and a power source); but they created each to use a piece of the sun: nuclear energy. Engineers have been building both weapons and power sources for centuries. But it was the degree of newness of these inventions or maybe the repercussions and consequences of any slight errors in judgment that was so disproportionate. Before, if a weapon or power source didn't work so well, the engineers and scientists would keep sniffing around until their curiosity was satisfied and came up with a newer version that did the task appropriately.

Newspaperman H. L. Mencken said, "What actually urges a scientist on, is not some idea of service but a boundless pathological thirst to open unknown doors, not the liberator releasing slaves, not the Good Samaritan lifting up the fallen, but a dog sniffing tremendously at an infinite number of ratholes."

Winter

All the ingredients for spontaneous combustion of a nuclear war were on hand by the time the wheels of *Keep 19* left the ground on that Monday morning, January 23, 1961. We had the world's largest standing army of strategic bombers, brim full of weapons that were hundreds of times more destructive than any weapon ever used in war. The weapons were carefully designed to perform most-efficiently; they were made from rare and magical materials created in the forges of nuclear reactors. Our most intelligent and gifted people built the weapons using the best and safest devices they knew of, but they were just that—devices built by men. We trained our sons and fathers to be brave and skilled professional warriors with faith in their country, a country that had just saved the world from despots, and we were ready to do it again. These men and women had the dedication and perseverance of our forefathers—it was in their DNA. We put them in the finest flying machine ever invented for all those purposes—the two-hundred-ton Boeing B-52. The unstoppable momentum of a new force—the combination of science, industry, ethos, and pride—brought together all of that equipment, manpower, and expertise. Then we built a massive pyramid controlled by the spoken word, communications from the conscience of man. There are people today who firmly believe that if just one of those *best devices made by man* had failed in that one bomb at Faro, logic would *not* have prevailed, we would *not* be thinking clearly; we would have delivered the fire, and we would have witnessed the horrors of a nuclear winter.

Final Thoughts

A scant 58 years before the Goldsboro crash, and just 128 miles away, the Wright brothers successfully launched their flimsy aircraft at Kitty Hawk, North Carolina. Millions visit the Wright Brothers National Memorial now, and the massive 60-foot monument on top of a 90-foot hill is very impressive. It is made from more than 1,200 tons of granite; it took years to build and was dedicated in 1932.

However, pilots are more impressed by standing at the spot nearby where the first flight actually took place, which is marked by a simple 6-foot-high bolder marked with a bronze plaque. Leading away to the north like runway markers is a series of 4 more smaller stones, at 120 feet, 175 feet, 200 feet, and 852 feet, each marking a landing spot of those four flights on December 17, 1903.

During a recent visit, I was out at the boulder and I asked a park ranger who was walking by, "How do you know this was the spot, the exact spot where the first flight left the ground?" I put my foot on the iron launch rail beside the stone and looked around at the acres of sand. "This is a big area. Why is the rock right here?"

"Because Orville said this was the spot," was the reply. "When this monument was dedicated in 1928 . . . before *that* monument was even planned," he gestured over his shoulder at the big stone colossus on the hill, "Orville came out here, took a look around, and said something very important. He said, 'Yep, this is the spot.'" It was obvious to the ranger that the real Wright brothers monument was this 6-foot-high bolder. That was really where *man first left planet Earth*. Right there.

In 2011 I drove Jack ReVelle to the spot on Shackleford Road where local people said the bomb was caught up in the trees, the first bomb that fell, caught by the parachute. He walked straight over to a gum tree beside a ditch, about a hundred feet north of the road, looked around, and said, "This is it." Right there was where he had disarmed a 3.8-megaton MK-39 thermonuclear weapon on the morning of January 24, 1961.

He wasn't as sure about the spot over on Big Daddy's Road, the place where the secondary is still buried. He said it all looked the same back then, nothing but snow on a big plowed field. But he was so focused on digging out that bomb, he wasn't aware of his surroundings at the buried bomb site. He knew where the bomb in the tree was, however. He even knew which tree it was. He had been there, fifty years before.

We now know the location of the buried bomb component. At least we know where the government's four-hundred-foot circle legal easement is located, based on the official land records in the Wayne County Court House.

We now stand about fifty years on this side of the Goldsboro Broken Arrow. We should be awed by how much aeronautical science and skill mankind has learned on both sides of that one point in time. If we measure a skill—for example, how fast man can travel—we can chart the growth: in two centuries we have gone from the speed of a horse, to a locomotive, to the speed of spacecraft. Likewise, weapons have gone from bayonets to bullets to *hell in a bucket*. We should remember how close we came to a nuclear winter back in 1961. We should also remember where that spot is and try to learn the lesson so that we don't repeat it.

Here is an old saying from the area where this all happened: We drink water from wells we did not dig. We eat food from fields we did not plow. We worship in churches we did not build, and we enjoy freedoms we did not earn. Let us remember those who came before us. We should feel grateful for these men who put themselves in harm's way for the security of generations yet to come.

Joel Dobson, 2011

The Return to the Bomb One Site After Fifty Years.
Photo by author.

Jack ReVelle was the explosive ordnance disposal officer who rendered safe this 3.8-megaton thermonuclear bomb in 1961.
Image courtesy USAF.

AFTERWORD
By Wilton W. Strickland, Lt. Col., USAF, (Retired)

For more than forty years after World War II and until the collapse of the Soviet Union in 1991, there was a period known as The Cold War. The United States and the Soviet Union, figuratively, held a very sharp-pointed *spear* to each other's throats. Those spears were in the form of very large nuclear arsenals capable of inflicting unimaginable holocaust and were guided by a policy of Mutually Assured Destruction (MAD)—an attack by one on the other would result in complete destruction of both.

For nearly sixteen years, during the period from February 1957 through October 1981, I lived on the very point of that American spear as a member of the US Air Force Strategic Air Command—first, for nearly three years as a maintenance crew chief on B-47 long-range nuclear bombers and later, for thirteen years, as an aircrew navigator and a radar navigator/bombardier on B-52s, the very long-range, heavy bombers that have been the mainstay of the nation's nuclear deterrent force for more than fifty-five years, along with land-based and submarine-launched intercontinental ballistic missiles. During most of my time in B-52s, I spent about every third week on ground alert, ready to take off at a moment's notice, and deliver nuclear weapons to targets in the Soviet Union. During my five thousand hours in flight on B-52s, I also flew several airborne alert (Chrome Dome) missions into the north polar and Mediterranean areas armed with nuclear weapons and, again, ready to quickly turn and strike targets in the Soviet Union.

This book is the tragic story of eight other men who were also on the point of that spear—the men of crew R-10 and *Keep 19*, the ill-fated B-52 from Seymour Johnson AFB, NC, that broke apart on approach to landing at Seymour Johnson on the cold, very early morning of January 24, 1961, which caused the two H-bombs aboard to separate from the aircraft as if they had been deliberately released, raining possible massive destruction onto the small farming community of Faro, NC.

I vaguely remember hearing about the accident soon after it happened in 1961, but I never delved into the details of it until the Air

Force brought me to the B-52 unit at Seymour Johnson in 1979. Since then I've read many articles about the accident, too often including misinformation and sensationalism. This book is the most comprehensive and complete work on the subject that I have seen. It also omits the misleading sensationalism that prevailed over the last fifty years. The author's open-mindedness, his search for the truth, and the recent declassification of certain government documents has resulted in this outstanding historical account of the incident.

Appendix A

The Crewmembers

Pilot	Walter Scott Tulloch	Major	45	AO726513	*San Diego, CA*
			born	15 Aug 1915	Phoenix, Arizona
			died	9 May 1992	San Diego, CA
			spouse	Elizabeth C.	
Copilot	Richard William Rardin	Captain	33	AO1856099	*San Antonio, TX*
			born	10 Mar 1927	Hamilton Co, Ohio
			died	5 July 1981	San Francisco, CA
			spouse	Charlie Belle Gainer	
EW	William R. Wilson	1/Lt	27	AO3054755	*(Somerville, NJ,*
			born 1933 +/- 1		*or Temple, TX, both are listed)*
Nav	Paul Edward Brown, Jr	Captain	37	AO759891	*Beardstown, IL*
			born	27 April 1923	IL
			died	29 April 1988	
RN	Eugene Shelton	Major	41	AO724231	*San Antonio, TX*
			born	15 May 1919	Bexar Co., TX
			died	24 Jan 1961	Goldsboro, NC
			spouse	Coloma M., "Rusty"	

Gunner	Francis Roger E. Barnish	TSgt	35		AF31415124	*Greenfield, MA*
			born	30 June 1925		Mass
			died	24 Jan 1961		Goldsboro, NC
			spouse	June F.		
EW	Eugene Holcombe Richards	Major	42		AO804873	*Toccoa, GA*
			born	18 June 1918		FL
			died	24 Jan 1961		Goldsboro, NC
			spouse	Sue C.		
3rd Pilot	Adam Columbus Mattocks	1/Lt	27		AO3072164	*Maysville, NC*
			born	9 Aug 1933		Onslow Co, NC
			spouse	Anne		

(Rank, age, and hometown of record at time of crash, 1961)

Appendix B

This Is What It Was Like: Major Tulloch's Narrative (1961)

A few months ago we were flying this big jet bomber, a B-52G, out over the Atlantic Ocean one night, and she developed trouble, which finally progressed to the point where an explosion shattered a wing. Most of us got out of her OK, but so many of my friends, even people who have flown for years during all sorts of conditions of war and peace, have asked me what it was like, that I would like to tell it as best I can in my own unskilled words. Many have endured much more harrowing experiences and real adventures have written hair-raising tales of happenings which leave us breathless. But to me, the real drama is the terse account by some ordinary Joe who was just doing his job and suddenly came to grips with real terror.

Frank, the gunner, had been shot down over Germany in WW II, been made a prisoner, but escaped to the American lines. Paul, the navigator, had survived two crashes during the same war. Dick, the copilot, was an ex-fighter jockey and test pilot who had survived three flamed out jets, which nearly took him with them. He did not talk about it much, but he was gray in his thirties. All the rest of us, except the very youngest had survived hundreds of hours of combat flying. What I'm trying to say is we were just a bunch of guys doing our job, and the last thing we wanted was for that plane to ~~come "unglued"~~ (strikethrough: sic) dump us out like dice out of a cup.

We were flying one of those exercises to train for the "Airborne Alert" posture. The airplane was loaded and ready to go to war by the simple procedure of turning her nose in the direction of the enemy and throwing a multitude of switches that cocked her bombs and weapons. You are up there for twenty-four hours tooling around in range of potential customers, and occasionally one of the jet tankers will come up and pump a few tons of fuel into the bomber just to keep her able to cover a good share of the earth's surface. Because of the long hours we had a third pilot along to take a turn at the controls, this bird can get out of hand in seconds and requires an alert eye. This young Lt. was not in a seat that would eject, and was to experience an escape that was little short of miraculous. Back in the defense section, a Major from Wing staff was also occupying one of those deadly spare seats that are not equipped with an ejection mechanism. He was an electronics warfare officer of wide experience and had volunteered to go along to help our defense team smooth out their operation. He was not lucky.

The first hint of trouble, like that first puff of smoke that precedes a forest fire, was when we were completing an in-flight refueling with one of our tanker aircraft. We had backed off to get set to take on the final few thousands of pounds of fuel that would top our tanks when the "boomer" on the tanker (often called Casey, because he lowers the refueling boom from the tanker into the receptacle on the bomber) called us and told us that we were losing a great deal of fuel out of the bottom of our right wing, just aft of one of the jet pods. There is a tremendous vent near the end of each wing to take care of over flow in case a valve should fail, but for a lot of fuel to be pouring out into the exhaust of the two jets was quite another matter. A quick check revealed that one of our main tanks was indeed losing thousands of gallons of fuel. Evidently it had split, or an inspection plate had come loose. Fuel pouring out into the open air at that altitude is scarcely combustible and most large aircraft are equipped to dump fuel in an emergency to lighten the load, so it did not appear to pose an immediate danger. Were rapidly approaching our home base, so I had the copilot call them and explain our difficulties, advise them that I intended to remain at altitude out over the ocean, in case anything happened, and that at dawn I wanted a chase plane to come up and check us over before we tried to land. In the meantime, I wanted our tanker to drop down below us and try to see what was wrong, but it was dark, and it is dangerous for a big plane to get too close, so he could not see much. The way the wing is swept back on the B-52, we could see nothing. It seemed a good idea to shut down the two jets adjacent to the leak, even though the tank was nearly drained by now. One of the rules of war is to be prepared for the worst, so I warned the crew to be ready to leave in an instant in case we found ourselves in what is known as an "untenable position."

Down in our Wing Headquarters things really came alive. Every Wing has a Command Post, manned by some very keen personnel who have telephone, Teletype, and radio contact with everyone up and down the whole SAC chain of command. In a few moments I was talking to our Wing Commander who was in his staff car, hurrying down to see that we got every bit of assistance possible, even to calling the people who built the airplane to get their views on what was wrong. The SAC Wing Commanders in my experience have, to a man, resembled tough football coaches faced with a crucial game. They can be as relaxed and charming as any other big executive on rare occasions but there are no seasons in the deadly game we are playing and the safety of our nation and the free world is at stake, so you had better know what you are doing and saying when your are around one of these gentlemen, or you won't be around long. Our Colonel is no exception, and I know that he had plenty of experts around him to make sure that we did not overlook anything. Our crew were all expert also, or we wouldn't have been trusted with a multimillion dollar aircraft loaded with more destructive power than most Generals commanded in by-gone wars, but I wanted any help they had to offer. It was my own lonely responsibility, and all decisions were up to me, as Aircraft Commander, but the Good Book says, "with good advice, make war," and under the complexities of modern operations, this is truer than ever. I particularly wanted to hear from the chief of our Standardization Crew. His job is similar to that of an Air Line's Chief Pilot. He had checked us out in these machines when we had reported to this base, and all of the other pilots shared my own high esteem of him. This was not because he was lenient, for he resembled nothing so much as a lean hard-boiled sheriff in the old frontier towns, who would drink beer with the boys, but shoot them down if they got out of line. We knew we had trouble, which was like a crouching tiger—soon it would spring.

Many pilots were like hypochondriacs about their airplanes. They are careful to the point of being fearful. They always look on the dark side. Caution has its merits, but carried too far, it has been responsible for people abandoning aircraft that could have been easily saved. We have always looked on the bright side. Besides, this bomber cost millions of dollars. In the Air Force we are intensely conscious of waste, and every officer is graded on what he can do to save the taxpayer dollar. It would have been a simple thing to just point the stricken plane's nose out to sea, and bail out before things got too tense, but we were determined to try to save her. However, she was getting worse each minute, for now the next big fuel tank had sprung a leak and was rapidly pouring its fuel out into the slipstream. The Wing Commander decided we should land as soon as possible even though the plane was still very heavy from the recent refueling and it was night. His wishes were revealed to us by a coastal radar sight, as we were circling out over the ocean, a safe distance from where the citizens slumbered peacefully in their beds. I concurred with the decision to land for I had studied a recent report of another bomber who had made it safely down under similar circumstances, but it had burst into flames on the runway, so I warned the crew to be ready to "make tracks" as soon as we could land and get stopped. Our main problem was to try to land without flying over anyone on the ground. Those folks down there were depending on us to defend them, not rain flaming death and destruction down on them in the middle of the night. I wanted to bail everyone out but the copilot and I, but we needed the navigators to guide us around the cities and towns on our way in. This was to cost the radar operator his life.

We lowered the ten wheels that comprise our landing gear while we were in the thin air of high altitude as there is much less chance of explosion there. Then we started down, and back to the base, threading our way cautiously around the cities, towns, and villages—I'd flown many a night bombing raid, and I never want to see that happen to an American city. When we got down to ten thousand feet they called us to check the airplane with full flaps down at that altitude, before landing it. In combat the rule had been to never lower the flaps if you had a damaged wing, so the experts must have decided that the wing was OK, and our only problem was the fuel leak. This did not seem too serious, as both tanks had drained themselves long before we started down. At our heavy weight without flaps we would have been landing at a terrific speed, so if the wing would stand it, it would be much better to make a normal landing with the flaps down, so we started them down. Had we put the flaps down at low altitude, as usual, it would have destroyed us all, for it triggered immediate, insurmountable trouble.

I'd told the copilot to tell them that the airplane seemed to handle OK with full flaps when there was a loud noise down under her like we had struck something and she started a violent roll to the left. We had no sooner got her out of that, and back on an even keel then there was an even worse noise, and she started trying to roll over to the right, and though fighting desperately we could not hold her. I ordered the crew to bail out. In this B-52G, only the pilots can see out—the others have no way of knowing what is going on, so someone called me back on intercom and said, "Did you say 'bail out'?" It is amazing that anyone would stop to double check at a time like this, but people had ejected by mistake before and our boys were tuned to a much higher state of discipline—not by me, but themselves. So I shouted into the intercom, "Yes! Bail Out!" There were a lot of muffled explosions which I at first thought were more trouble, but when, finally, the copilot ejected and the shell which fires the seat out went off, I realized that this was a good sound—the lads were firing their seats off, and were safely away. I was putting up the fight of my life, using every trick I had been taught or learned in thousands of hours of flying and many trips over enemy targets, trying to hold the big beast from rolling over on her back, until the extra crewmembers could dive out the holes left in the bottom of the aircraft when the navigators on the lower deck had ejected. It was in vain, for the big ship got up into a vertical bank, and started plunging toward the earth. This had all happened in seconds, but now, all was lost—regretfully I let go of the controls and fired my seat.

The aircraft was inverted, and I was hanging in my seat belt, which I had neglected to pull real tight, so the seat got a couple of inches start and hit my behind with a terrible jolt and I found myself tumbling through the blast, pummeled and wrenched in all directions. It was like when you catch one of those big breakers at the beach: it overpowers you and finally flings you stunned and gasping up on the beach. My crash helmet and oxygen mask were torn off, but the automatic devices opened the seat belt and the seat fell away, and the parachute opened smoothly. I was surrounded by flaming pieces of wreckage which the plane had shed in its mad plunge and in danger of dropping into the holocaust on the ground where it had struck, but the feeling of floating down in an open chute is among the finest physical sensations I have ever enjoyed, I can see why people do it for sport, and it was made doubly enjoyable when I viewed the flaming death I had so narrowly escaped. Surely the boys had all made it out safely. I had heard their seats fire, and it would take just a second for the extra crewmembers to dive out after the navigators ejected. I could see someone now, floating down in his parachute, and I shouted to him hoping we could get together on the ground, but he hung there like a rag doll, and did not answer. Much later I found that this was the radar navigator. He had ejected safely but something had struck him in the head and killed him. The reason he did not answer was that he was already on his way to a better world.

Suddenly I found myself plunging into treetops and arranged my arms and legs to protect myself. It seemed a shame that such a delightful ride should end with such a rude jolt, but there I was safely on the ground. My own most deadly peril was to come much later.

I made the usual check for broken parts, unbuckled my chute, took a sighting on the North Star, hung up my chute where I could find it should I need it again, and set out to find a farm with a telephone where I could phone to report in and find out if everyone was down safely. As I tried one direction after another only to fall into pools of freezing water, I was surprised to find myself lying with my face in the mud. I had blacked out. Obviously I was in the middle of a swamp and exhausting myself in my struggles. It was freezing cold, and my teeth were chattering, so I made my way back to my chute and rolled up in it to get warm. When the rescue helicopters started coming over, I got up and made a feeble attempt to signal them by waving the chute, as I had lost my flashlight and matches when the trees ripped my flying suit on the way down through them. I soon gave up, for I knew I could get out as soon as it grew light, and I was starting to black out again. I rolled up in that good old chute again and soon felt better physically, but my anxiety about the others was mounting. If someone were really hurt, and in a swamp like I was, it might be hard to find him.

At the first light of dawn, I made my way out to a road, got a ride to a farmhouse with a phone, called the Wing Command Post to report in, and find out if the rest of the boys were all OK. The spare pilot was my main worry, for he had been up on the flight deck helping us with circuit breakers we could not reach, and I was not sure that he had got down to the lower deck in time to dive out after the navigator. It developed that he had still been on the flight deck, and when the plane went over on her back he dove out the topside after I ejected. Ordinarily, the fin and rudder would have hit him, but it had snapped off so he was saved, and landed right in a farm yard and did not even have to walk. They assured me that the others would soon turn up, now that it was light. I was to get a ride over to the crash scene where our Commander was, and he would get me back to the base. I phoned my wife, who wept with relief. No words can express what the girls go through at a time like this. As I write these words, a crew I flew with for months has vanished over the North Atlantic without a trace. To watch the young wives wait with waning hope while trying to comfort their small children is heartbreaking.

The crash scene was ghastly, but my heart welled with gratitude that, although there were farmhouses in the area, no person or stick of property had been destroyed. The kindly farmer who let me use his phone, and gave me a ride over there had an expression of shock on his face as he viewed the terrible destruction, and considered that his own small house was only a mile away. I reported to our Wing Commander, who tried to reassure me about the rest of the crew, and had me hustled off to the hospital. I must have been in worse shape than I suspected. My real ordeal stall lay before me.

In the hospital I blacked out three more times, and crashed to the floor before the corpsmen could catch me. They were glad to get me into a bed where they set up a round-the-clock watch, until the Doctors were sure I was out of danger. I was told that the others were being collected and were in a room down the hall. I even thought I heard some of them outside my door. Relief and exhaustion helped me to drift off into sleep. Next morning, when I kept insisting that I wanted to see them I was told the grim truth—three of them had perished.

The next night, I was alone with my grief. This loss sorely afflicted me. The radar operator was a burly Texan, with a fine crop of three boys and a little daughter, and devoted wife. The Major from the Wing Staff was one of the most popular officers in Wing. Something had delayed his dive out to safety, and when the airplane got over on its back, he was doomed. His wife and son can hardly bare their loss. Frank, the gunner, who had survived so much had started to fire his seat, and had blown the escape hatch off, but then something had gone wrong. The few seconds' delay had been fatal. He left three children and a sick wife.

I was stricken with remorse. The beating I had taken, coupled with this news, destroyed an equanimity that had carried me through a life of hardship. Why had I tried to save that cursed plane? According to the newspapers few seem to worry much about a few million dollars of government money. And I had lost, not only the airplane, but also three men I loved like brothers. Black despair dragged me down to the depths, and waves of grief swept over me. As a lad, my Sunday School teacher had been a retired General, and he had inoculated me with the highest ideals about life and military service. I could see him standing trim and erect as though he was addressing his troops, and I could almost hear him saying, "The Captain should go down with his ship." I'd thought I was the last one out, but I had survived, and three had been lost. The ancient scripture I had learned in my youth came ringing through my troubled mind—"Greater love hath no man than to lay down his life for his friends." But my friends were gone, and I was safe. Feebly I struggled in the grip of despair that could bring on a shattered mind. I knew I needed help from the angels and one was right down the hall—I rang for the nurse.

My angel was a little slip of a girl who looked like someone's kid sister, and when she saw my face, she looked scared. I begged for something that would knock me out and help me escape my horrible thoughts, but the doctor was off delivering a baby and orders were that I could be given nothing 'til some tests they were running were finished. She looked troubled, and finally said brightly, "I'll give you a back rub, perhaps that will get you to sleep." Anything was better than being left alone in this hell of despair so I eagerly acquiesced. Gradually my troubled mind returned to normal, and I drifted into a healing sleep.

Now, when I roll our big bomber out on the runway for takeoff, just before I reach out my hand to advance the eight throttles that will send her rushing off into the night, I think of all those other hands that helped me back to a useful life. Tender hands in the hospital, hands at home that were clasped in prayer through a long night, comradely hands on the flight line that welcomed me back to duty, the hands of superiors that gave me a reassuring slap on the back and put me back in a cockpit where I loved to be. And all the hands across our nation, working to build a better life for all Americans, and yet have enough left over for all the empty hands in the world. It steadies my own hand.

Lieutenant Colonel Walter Scott Tulloch continued to fly the BUFF until he retired, on February 27, 1967. His last currency flight was January 18, 1967, one month before his retirement. He had over 26 years of service with 6,740 flying hours, 458 of them in combat. He was awarded the Distinguished Flying Cross and the Air Medal with Three Oak Leaf Clusters. He died of cancer on May 9, 1992, in San Diego, California, where his widow, Betty, still lives. She is eighty-five-years-old. JD

Appendix C

Findings of Accident Board
[*With descriptive notes*]

AF Form 14, B-52G, 58-187

1. The primary cause of this accident was materiel failure in that a fatigue crack in the #2 panel of the lower wing skin occurred at wing station 556 of the right wing, causing a major fuel leak in the #3 and #4 fuel tanks.

2. A contributing cause factor was also material failure in that the already weakened right wing separated from the aircraft following flap extension.

3. T.O. [Technical Order] 1B-52G-637 (ECP 951-5), requiring depot level compliance, was scheduled for 5 May 1961 during High Stress II modification. Compliance with this technical order would have prevented the failure of the #2 panel of the right wing lower skin.

4. The fact that a B-52G wing had experienced a similar failure during cyclic testing was not known at the operating level.

5. The present flight manual does not provide adequate guidance for major fuel leaks and fails to point out the fact that some structural damage is always associated with a large wing tank fuel leak.

6. The aircraft was directed into landing configuration because of concern over fire hazard accompanied by lateral control considerations, prior to detailed analysis of the emergency being completed by Boeing Airplane Company and while several hours of fuel remained aboard the aircraft.

7. In order to maintain near normal lateral balance for landing, the recommended fuel usage procedures contained in T.O. 1B-52G-1 were not followed.

8. The UHF radio in the Command Post was unsatisfactory during a major portion of the emergency.

9. Information recorded on the Command Post tape was of limited value in establishing sequence of events, in that it was turned off during portions of the emergency and the time was not periodically recorded.

10. The VGH Gust Recorder in the aircraft was not sufficiently protected to conserve the information.

11. The Staff EWO [Major Richards], occupying the IN seat [Instructor Navigator seat, at the back of The Hole], was unable to reach either of the two downward hatches.

12. The gunner [TSgt Barnish] was unable to find and/or pull the catapult trigger to complete his ejection sequence.

13. The Radar-Navigator [Major Shelton] was jerked against his ejection seat when the parachute inflated and after his helmet was lost, resulting in fatal injury.

14. Surviving crewmembers did not pull down their helmet visors and did not have chin straps tightly fastened.

15. Two survival kit life rafts were inflated inadvertently and could have resulted in unsatisfactory parachute opening or a fatal injury.

Appendix D

Table of Component Behavior, Fusing, and Firing System

MIC No.	Component	Bomb #1	Bomb #2
	Arming Wires	Pulled	Pulled
845	Pulse Generator	Actuated	Actuated
543	Timer	Ran Down (deleted)	Ran 12-15 Sec.
832	Differential Pressure Switch	All Contacts Closed	2 Contacts Closed
640	Low Voltage Thermal Battery	Actuated	Actuated
772	Arm-Safe Switch	Safe	(See Sect 5)
1-A	Tritium Reservoir	Full	Full
641	High Voltage Thermal Battery	Actuated	Not Actuated
788	Rotary Safing Switch	Not Operated	Destroyed
730	X Unit	Not Charged	Not Charged
615	Nose Crystals	Crushed	Crushed

Source: *Speer Report*, February 16, 1961

[End of Report]

Appendix E

Known Broken Arrows
(Declassified as of 1980)

In addition to the Goldsboro Broken Arrow there are thirty-five additional accidents that involved nuclear weapons that were released by the Department of Defense and Department of Energy in 1983. Here are the thirty-six as reported by Maggelet and Oskins in their book, Broken Arrow, The Declassified History of U.S. Nuclear Weapons Accidents.

In their newest book, they report at least a total of sixty Broken Arrows.

Date	Aircraft	Location
February, 13, 1950	B-36	Pacific Ocean
April 11, 1950	B-29	Manzano Base, NM
July 13, 1950	B-50	Lebanon, OH
August 5, 1950	B-29	Fairfield-Suisun AFB, CA
November 10, 1950	B-50	Outside US, St. Lawrence River
March 10, 1956	B-47	Mediterranean Sea
July 27, 1956	B-47	Overseas Base
May 27, 1957	B-36	Kirtland AFB, NM
July 28, 1957	C-124	Atlantic Ocean
October 11, 1957	B-47	Homestead AFB, FL
January 31, 1958	B-47	Overseas Base
February 5, 1958	B-47	Savannah River, GA
March 11, 1958	B-47	Florence, SC
November 4, 1958	B-47	Dyess AFB, TX
November 26, 1958	B-47	Chennault AFB, LA

January 18, 1959	F-100	Pacific Base
July 6, 1959	C-124	Barksdale AFB, LA
September 25, 1959	P-5M	Off Whidbey Island, WA
October 15, 1959	B-52, KC-135	Hardinsburg, Kentucky
June 7, 1960	Bomarc	McGuire AFB, NJ
January 24, 1961	B-52	Goldsboro, NC
March 14, 1961	B-52	Yuba City, CA
November 13, 1963	Storage Igloo	Medina Base, TX
January 13, 1964	B-52	Cumberland, MD
December 5, 1964	ICBM	Ellsworth AFB, SD
December 8, 1964	B-58	Bunker Hill AFB, IN
October 11, 1965	C-124	Wright-Patterson AFB, OH
December 5, 1965	A-4	At Sea, Pacific Ocean
January 17, 1966	B-52/KC-135	Palomares, Spain
January 21, 1968	B-52	Thule, Greenland
Spring, 1968	Submarine	At Sea, Atlantic Ocean
September 19, 1980	Titan II ICBM	Damascus, AK

In 1962, there were four Thor IRBM explosions involving nuclear warheads on Johnston Island, Pacific Ocean:

June 3	Thor-Bluegill
June 20	Thor-Starfish
July 25	Thor-Bluegill Prime
Oct 15	Thor-Bluegill Double Prime

It should be noted that there has never been even a partial, inadvertent US nuclear detonation reported. All detonations involved conventional high explosives only.

Appendix F

Bomb Locations at Faro:

Bomb No. 1, the "bomb in the trees" was on Shackleford Road, SR 1616, .67 miles east of the intersection with Big Daddy's Road, Faro.

Lat 35° 29.526 N, Long 77° 50.808 N

The location is based on eyewitness reports, including the explosive ordnance disposal officer.

Bomb No. 2, the "buried bomb," was on Big Daddy's Road, SR 1532, .4 miles south of intersection with Shackleford Road, Faro.

Lat 35° 29.628 N, Long 77° 51.497 W

The location is based on eyewitness reports and the legal deed description of the 400-foot-wide circle (200 ft radius) easement, which is now owned by the US Government. The site is not fenced or marked, and is 420 feet NE (320° magnetic) from centerline of Big Daddy's Road.

If you go there, please do not trespass. This is active farmland. The good folks of Faro have had enough damage done to their land.

How I Located the *Lost Bomb* of Goldsboro:

The site is not marked or fenced. As of 2011 there is nothing there but a cultivated field with a small, overgrown cemetery near the center. By using tools such as Google Earth to measure distance, one would need a GPS receiver, maybe a compass, and the following information:

The legal easement for the two-hundred-foot radius circle is recorded on the deed books in the Wayne County Courthouse (Book 581, pp 589-91, State of NC, County of Wayne, October 13, 1962) as follows:

"All of that area in the form of a circle, having a radius of 200 feet, with the center point of radius located through the following traverse: From a common corner to the lands of heirs of Charles T. Davis, Sr. and land of J. A. Edmundson, located on the centerline of N. C. State Road 1534 and approximately 2,135 feet northeasterly from the centerline of

Nahunta Swamp; thence along the centerline of N. C. State Road 1534, N 49 degrees 28' E, 835.56 feet; thence leaving the centerline of N.C. State Road 1534, N 40 degrees 32' W, 420 feet to the center point of radius, and containing 2.88 acres, more or less."

Here's how to use that somewhat bewildering information:

1.) For the "centerline of the swamp," see the following graphic. Start at the Nahunta Swamp where it is crossed by NC State Route 1534 (Big Daddy's Road). The bridge is about 2 miles southwest of Faro, NC. The legal description of the swamp at the point where the bridge crosses it, actually starts at the northern end of the bridge and extends northeast only about 700 feet. You have to estimate the centerline of the swamp, then go 2,135 feet northeasterly (toward Faro) on the road. That will bring you to:

2.) The common corner of the Davis and Edmundson land, which apparently was a significant landmark to surveyors.

3.) From that point, continue northeast for another 835.6 feet along the centerline of the road (49° magnetic). You just passed where the main wreckage lay in the middle of the road in 1961. This brings you to the spot to place your virtual golf ball.

4.) Look left 90° relative to the road. You will be looking northwest, a magnetic heading of 320°.

(Or, in the wording of surveyors: N 40 degrees 32' W. This actually means 40.5 degrees west of magnetic north, which makes it 320° by compass.) Four hundred twenty feet along that line of sight from the center of the road is the center of the circular easement.

Stare at the horizon for a minute, the way the guys in the hole did in 1961.

The GPS coordinates of the spot on the edge of the road are:

Lat 35° 29.579 N, Long 77° 51.440 W

5.) If you could hit a reasonably good 420-feet, or 140-yard golf shot, (a six iron for me), you would maybe hit the approximate center of the easement circle. That's where Bomb Number 2 hit that night, and where the core is now: 180 feet down. Under the circle of "2.88 acres, more or less."

Joel Dobson 163

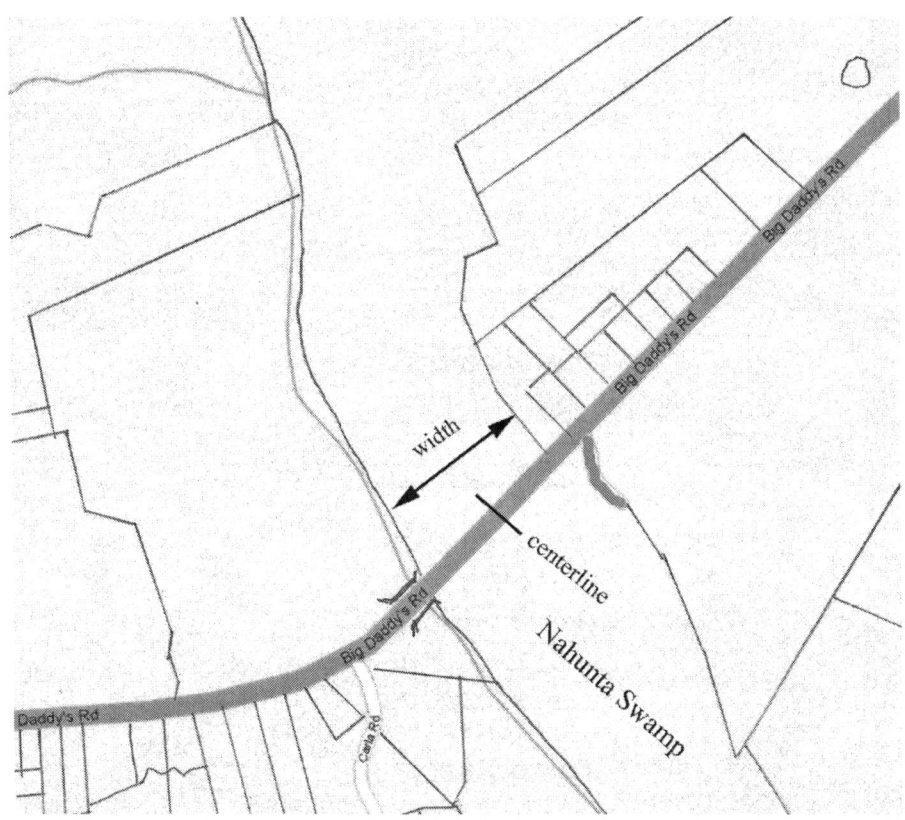

Nahunta Swamp Bridge, Lower Left.
The government's four-hundred-foot circle easement of the bomb two site is in the upper right corner.
Image by author.

NOTES

General

" . . . Largest man-made disaster in history . . . " came from *World Armaments and Disarmament: Stockholm International Peace Research Institute Yearbook* (1977) 58-78. The Institute made the statement in 1977, and it was probably influenced by an erroneous call by Dr. Ralph Lapp sixteen years earlier. Dr. Lapp was a well-known atomic scientist and the former executive director of the Department of Defense's Atomic Research and Development Board. He was the man who coined the phrase *The China Syndrome*. In his 1961 book *Kill and Overkill: The Strategy of Annihilation* (New York: Basic Books, Inc., 1961) 127, he stated that the Goldsboro bomb was twenty-four megatons. That would have been bigger than anything in the US nuclear inventory.

MK-39. Chuck Hansen, the late civilian nuclear historian, was the first to identify the bomb in the trees as the MK-39 based on published photographs. According to a SAC weapons archive, the MK-39 would produce a minimum of two and a maximum of four megatons. A controversy began when *two to four* megatons was mistakenly identified in the press as twenty-four megatons, but that was never true. While at the University of North Carolina at Chapel Hill giving a presentation about the Goldsboro incident, Mr. Hansen stated that he did not believe that Dr. Lapp was being disingenuous with his report of twenty-four megatons, rather it was a misplacement of a decimal point. Even a 2.4-megaton bomb would exceed the yield of all munitions (outside of testing) ever detonated in the history of the world by TNT, gunpowder, and the Hiroshima and Nagasaki blasts combined. (Calculation by Dr. Ralph Lapp and others, and reconfirmed by Chuck Hansen, as reported by Scott Hardy, in his thesis *The Broken Arrow Of Camelot: An Analysis Of The 1961 B-52 Crash And Loss Of Nuclear Weapon In Faro, North Carolina*, 24.)

Part I.

Notes to Chapter 1. The Crew and Their Plane

Information on Readiness Crew R-10 came from *AF Form 14*, "Report of Aircraft Accident," obtained through FOIA, October 2010.

. . . twelve bombers in the air . . . is an excerpt from Barbara Moran's book *The Day We Lost the H-Bomb*.

"B-52, workhorse: Details of the Aircraft and Its Performance" came *Boeing B-52: A Documentary History* by Colonel Walter Boyne and from the *History of the B-52 Stratofortress* offered as published work on www.GlobalSecurity.org.

Details about SAC's performance in the Cuban Crisis came from personal experience and *SAC Operations in the Cuban Crisis of 1962. Historical Study No. 90, Vol 1*, 48.

Comparison of SAC to Standard Oil came from Doug Keeney's book *15 Minutes: General Curtis LeMay and the Countdown to Nuclear Annihilation*, 116.

The Men on *the sharp end*. Information on Major Tulloch came from his wife Betty, a spry lady who was very appreciative of the people of Seymour Johnson and the community of the Goldsboro area. When we had the commemorative dinner at the Faro Fire Department, she sent a gracious note of appreciation thanking the volunteer firemen, now and then, who had put their lives on the line, without pay, to protect their community. Other information comes from area newspapers and *AF Form 14*.

Frank Barnish's POW Experience came from the Kassel Mission Web site www.KasselMission.com and from Frank's cousin, Jerry Barnish.

Details of the Radar Navigator's Duties came from interviews with Lt. Col. Wilton Strickland, USAF, (Retired).

Information On the "two-man" policy came from *One Minute to Midnight: Kennedy, Khrushchev, and Castro on the Brink of Nuclear War* by Michael Dobbs (excerpted below). (New York: Alfred A. Knopf, 2008.)

There were other military situations within the Department of Defense where the two-man policy was modified. When single seat aircraft were equipped with nuclear weapons, they were locked by PALS, Permissive Action Links, and the pilot did not received the unlock code until en route to the target. The only exception to the policy was in time of war, when an enemy attack was considered imminent.

That was the situation a year after the *Keep 19* crash, during the Cuban Missile Crisis. Here are two of many examples. The Commander In Chief of NORAD wanted F-106 fighter-interceptor jets loaded and dispersed to municipal airports all over the country, ready to intercept Soviet bombers and not be sitting ducks. The jets were equipped with 1.5-kiloton *Genie* air-to-air missiles, which was considered by some to be the "dumbest weapons system ever purchased." It wasn't designed to hit a target, just put it near an enemy aircraft, and it would blow up whatever was in the vicinity through the sheer force of the blast. Some of the F-106s went to municipal airports that lacked adequate nuclear storage facilities. One crash-landed when the drag chute failed to deploy—with the nuclear missile aboard.

Also during the Cuban Missile Crisis the 613th Tactical Fighter Squadron stationed in Incirlik, Turkey, was permitted to load thermonuclear bombs into F-100 Super Sabre fighter-bombers, which were not yet secured by electronic locking systems. The aircraft were responsible for covering thirty-seven *high priority* Soviet bloc targets, mostly East German airfields. The squadron commander later said, "Nuclear safety was so loose, it jars your imagination. In retrospect, there were some guys you wouldn't trust with a .22 rifle, much less a thermonuclear bomb."

Broken Arrow Reports on single-seat aircraft is an excerpt from *Broken Arrows, Vol. II* by Maggelet and Oskins. (lulu.com, 2010). Excerpt below.

> There were two single-seat aircraft Broken Arrows reported in the 1980 DOD release:
>
> In 1959, a parked F-100 at a Pacific base caught fire with a MK-7 attached.
>
> In 1965, an A-4 with a MK-43 accidentally rolled off an elevator on the carrier USS Tikonderoga in the Pacific Ocean. The aircraft, weapon, and pilot were lost.

". . . going 390 knots with our hair on fire . . . " is an excerpt from *15 Minutes: General Curtis LeMay and the Countdown to Nuclear Annihilation* by Douglas Keeney. (New York: St. Martin's Press, 2011.)

Water use on B-52 takeoff came from an interview with Pete Seberger.

The description of spoiler controls came from interviews with BUFF Master Crew Chief Mike Meacher.

"The spoilers took some getting used to." The quote is excerpted from "The Dawn of Discipline," by Colonel Walter Boyne. (*Air & Space/Smithsonian*, July 2009.)

Notes to Chapter 2. The Mission

All details of the mission came from *AF Form 14, (nkd)*. "Report of Aircraft Accident, January 24, 1961," interviews with Adam Mattocks, and Major Tulloch's narrative.

The Wright Field Training Exercise description came from *15 Minutes: General Curtis LeMay and the Countdown to Nuclear Annihilation* by Doug Keeney. (New York: St. Martin's Press, 2011), 55.

Information on Curtis LeMay came from the Strategic Air Command official Web site, http://www.StrategicAirCommand.com

Information on The Maxwell Conference came from *15 Minutes: General Curtis LeMay and the Countdown to Nuclear Annihilation* by Doug Keeney. (New York: St. Martin's Press, 2011), 52.

Nuclear Bomb Explosion Device information: ibid, 237.

"Atlas probability of successful launch: Zero." ibid, 239.

"Florence Broken Arrow" information is based on Luke Dittrich's article, "Perfectly Understandable Mistake." (*Esquire* Magazine, May 2005.)

"The ICBMs were not designed to ride out a strike." This quote is an excerpt from *15 Minutes: General Curtis LeMay and the Countdown to Nuclear Annihilation* by Doug Keeney. (New York: St. Martin's Press, 2011), 174.

Notes on The Last Three Hours and Six Minutes of *Keep 19*

" . . . one refueling every 6.8 minutes . . . " details came from Doug Keeney's *15 Minutes,* 253, and from information provided by members of the Order of the Daedalians, Kitty Hawk Flight, Seymour Johnson Air Force Base, Goldsboro, North Carolina, on a personal visit May 12, 2011.

"Major Tulloch asked to get a chase plane ready . . . " All quotes came from his personal flight records, as loaned by his wife, Betty Tulloch in 2010, and from his personal narrative about the crash, which is attached as Appendix B.

Mattocks' quotes and experiences came from personal interviews. (2010 and 2011.)

" . . . They were now having to use excessive trim." This quote is an excerpt from the "Official Observer's Report."

" . . . ARAC 58 radio was inoperative, fatigue crack, and repair depot info." Is an excerpt from *AF Form 14*, "Accident Report."

Information on "Fuel Gushers" came from the Global Security Web site http://www.GlobalSecurity.org/wmd/systems/b-52.htm.

Fuel Clamp Failure. Herbert Marx, better known as Zeppo, one of the original five Marx Brothers, invented the Marman clamp. He was in seven of the Marx Brothers movies, including *Monkey Business, Horse Feathers,* and *Duck Soup.* He was the founder of Marman Aerospace Products of Inglewood, California. This tidbit was found in the column, "Oldies & Oddities: Zeppo's Gizmo" by Nick D'Alto. (*Air & Space/Smithsonian magazine*, September 2008.)

No one knows what type of clamps were used on the *Keep 19* aircraft. But it is obvious that something very important failed in order to cause such a large fuel leak. Here is a discussion of fuel clamp history, as summarized by Global Security (http://www.GlobalSecurity.org):

> Fuel leaks, occurring in the B-52Fs and preceding B-52Gs, proved difficult to stop. The problem manifested itself from the start. Marman clamps, the flexible fuel couplets interconnecting fuel lines between tanks, broke down on several occasions during the first few weeks of B-52 operation. This caused fuel gushers that obviously created serious flying hazards. Blue Band, a September 1957 project, put new clamps (CF-14s) in all B-52s. Depot assistance field teams did the retrofit well, but Blue Band did not work. The CF-14 aluminum clamps soon showed signs of stress corrosion and were likely to fall after 100 days of service. Highly concerned, the Air Force and Boeing began replacing the aluminum clamps with a Boeing-developed stainless steel strap clamp, the CF-17. Hard Shell, a high-priority retrofit program, put CF-17 clamps in all in-service B-52s. Completed in January 1958, the Hard Shell retrofit was not a fool-proof solution.

Bail Out Procedures and Details came from the USAF flight manual, *Dash-One*, and from personal conversations with BUFF guys.

"This is an intercepting turn of 60°, somewhat sharper than similar intercepting turns for civilian aircraft." This comment is based on an Air Traffic Controller's Table for final approach course interception. It states a recommended maximum interception angle of 20° if the distance to the approach gate is less than two miles, and 30° if two miles or more. The reason: the sharper the intercept turn, the steeper the banking of the aircraft which puts more stress on the wing. (Machado, 84). However, an approach turn of 60° is not at all considered unusual for a Boeing B-52, according to BUFF pilots. But with all the other damage to this airplane, this turn proved catastrophic.

" . . . the beast was rolling over on her back . . ." is an excerpt from Major Tulloch's narrative. (Appendix B)

"Mattocks and the simulator" and the bail out came from Adam Mattocks.

Notes to Chapter 3. The Bail Out

Bill Wilson and Dick Rardin's accounts came from J. Sedgewick's article "Bombs Over Goldsboro" from This Month in North Carolina History Archives, UNC Libraries, North Carolina Collection.

Survival kit and life raft information came from an interview with Staff Sergeant Michael Thomas of the Egress Section of the 371 TRS Training Squadron, Seymour Johnson Air Force Base, Goldsboro, North Carolina.

" . . . (Major Tulloch) hanging by his seat belt." This information came from Major Tulloch's son, Scott Tulloch, in an interview. (December 2010)

" . . . The lads were firing their seats and were safely away." This is an excerpt from Major Tulloch's narrative. (Appendix B)

"At base housing Betty Tulloch had been awakened . . . " came from interviews with Betty Tulloch. (2010 and 2011)

The details of Mattock's escape came from interviews with Adam Mattocks.

Anne Mattock's story was told to the author in interviews.

Notes to Chapter 4. The Crash Site

Personal stories about the crash came from interviews with Billy Reeves, Earl and Mary Lancaster, Rudolph Tyndall, Evan Keel, C. T. Davis, and Morris Cruise, all were eyewitnesses.

"It was eerie as hell . . ." is a Eugene Price quote from Gary Hanauer's article "The Story Behind the Pentagon's Broken Arrow." (*Mother Jones* Magazine, April 1981.)

Information on the Elroy Fire Department experience came from interviews with historian Evan Keel.

". . . procedures known as *Moist Mop* . . ." is an excerpt from *The Day We Lost the H-Bomb* by Barbara Moran (2009) and from SAC *Historical Study #109*, 288.

". . . .His wife's right side 'just burned and burned'" came from an interview with Dick Manley, USAF, (Retired). (2011)

"Jack, I've got a real one for you," came from interviews with Dr. Jack B. ReVelle. (2011)

". . . highlight was the mess tent at midnight . . . " came from an interview with Guy Altizer.

" . . . We've found the ARM/SAFE switch—and it's on ARM!" came from an interview with Dr. Jack B. ReVelle .

Information on "General Loper's letter" came from *15 Minutes: General Curtis LeMay and the Countdown to Nuclear Annihilation* by Doug Keeney. (New York: St. Martin's Press, 2011), 246.

"X Personnel, and W-7" information came from the Government Document: "Seymour Johnson Air Force Base Accident, Goldsboro, NC, W-7-2717, February 20, 1961" written by T. T. Scolman and D. R. Smith.

". . . the weapon fish-tailed in the earth . . . " came from an interview with Dr. Jack B. ReVelle.

DOD Directive 5230.16, "right to lie," information came from *Broken Arrow: The Declassified History of U.S. Nuclear Weapons Accidents Vol I,* by Maggelet and Oskins. (lulu.com, 2007)

"93,000 cubic yards of dirt was removed." This information came from T. A. Loving Company.

". . . many fifty-five-gallon metal drums were buried there . . . " came from an interview with Rudolph Tyndall. (February 2011)

Information on the government's easement came from an interview with C. T. Davis. (February 8, 2011)

Information on the missing secondary at Faro and other general information about the secondary came from Chuck Hansen who has done extensive research on this and many other nuclear accidents and events. His research papers were donated to the National Security Archive at George Washington University, Washington, DC. He once said that he had been investigated many times by the FBI for possible security violations, but they always concluded that everything he reported had been properly declassified.

Goldsboro or Faro? The location of this Broken Arrow is identified both ways in this work. The Department of Defense used the name Goldsboro based on the easiest recognizable place. Faro is used for the accident site itself when local references are used. (By the way, it's pronounced Fay-ro.)

The Gravesites. I found the name Frank Barnish in a relative's inquiry on a Web page concerning World War II POWs. The Web page was about the Kassel Mission, a little known US Air Corps disaster in World War II. By using an online search for military gravesites, I found that Sergeant Barnish was buried in the National Cemetery in Raleigh, which I visited. I shared all this information with his relatives in Massachusetts, who were most appreciative, especially for the information as to how he died. His cousin, Jerry Barnish, provided photographs.

Frank's gravestone shows him as being a member of the Ninety-seventh Bomb Wing, which was never assigned to Seymour Johnson as far as I can find. The *Accident Report (AF Form 14)* shows all crewmembers as being assigned to the 4241st Strategic Wing, Eighth Air Force. The gravestones of the other two casualties show the 4241st. The reason the Ninety-seventh is listed on Frank's stone is unclear.

There were incorrect rumors among the local people at Faro as to how Major Shelton died. One was that he survived the explosion but froze to death in a tree before he was discovered. The tree was two miles due east of the crash site, but over four miles away by road, and in a swamp. Another rumor said he died by being impaled on the tree. The fact is, his helmet's chin strap was not fastened tight enough and his helmet came off when his parachute inflated, and he was jerked against the ejection seat, causing fatal head injuries. There is no mention on his death certificate of injuries from being impaled by a tree, or from exposure. Major Shelton is buried at Fort Sam Houston National Cemetery in San Antonio. He enlisted in 1940, at Fort Sam Houston, on the same grounds, at a place less than a mile from where he is buried.

There was no record of Major Richards being buried in any national military cemetery. After searching for a civilian gravesite of Major Eugene Richards from Toocon, Georgia (the way it was spelled in several newspaper accounts), and with no results, I finally realized there is no Toocon, Georgia. However, there is a Toccoa, Georgia. My sister-in-law, Linda, a retired librarian from Kalamazoo, Michigan, always told me, "If you want to find out something, ask a librarian." So I did, and quickly found Major Richards' gravesite in Toccoa, thanks to Michelle Austin of the Toccoa-Stephens County Library and Judy Thomason of the Acree-Davis Funeral Home in Toccoa.

In 2010 we visited the gravesites of the three casualties in Raleigh, San Antonio, and Toccoa. Tokens were left at each site: a small stone from a North Carolina river, a tiny garland of green pine needles, and a SAC emblem from the museum in Nebraska.

Notes to Chapter 5. The Chance of Nuclear Detonation

How Big Were Those Bombs: MK-39, Mod 2. This information came from the nuclear bomb chart found at the Strategic Air Command Web site.

(www.Strategic-Air-Command.com/weapons/nuclear_bomb_chart.htm)

". . . each bomb was twenty-four megatons," is an excerpt from *Kill and Overkill: The Strategy of Annihilation* by Ralph Lapp. (Basic Books, 1962), 127.

"Two hundred sixty times the Hiroshima bomb." Information on how that number was calculated came from the Strategic Air Command Web site. (www.Strategic-Air-Command.com/weapons/nuclear_bombchart.htm) The Hiroshima *Little Boy* was between 12 and 18 kilotons. At 3.8 megatons, each MK-39 would be the equivalent factor of 211 to 317 Hiroshima bombs depending on which *Little Boy* figure used, or an average of 264.

A differing opinion came from *15 Minutes: General Curtis LeMay and the Countdown to Nuclear Annihilation* by Doug Keeney, 159. That careful calculation [from SAC] is different from the 1952 Operation Redwing test at Bikini. There, a 3.8-megaton device was estimated to be equal "roughly two thousand times the size of the Hiroshima bomb."

"Half life of Plutonium-239 is over 24,000 years . . . Uranium, four billion years." This information comes from the Nuclear Weapons Archive and from *The Day We Lost the H-Bomb* by Barbara Moran, 145.

Bomb Schematic, size, and shape of primary was described by Dr. Jack B. ReVelle. (2011)

". . . They finally solved it with the study of hydrodynamics . . . " is an excerpt from *Dark Sun: The Making of the Hydrogen Bomb* by Richard Rhodes. (New York: Simon & Schuster, 1995), 117.

". . . MK-39 secondary has an estimated total weight of at least two hundred pounds . . . " came from in interview with Dr. Jack B. ReVelle.

". . . Teller found it would take a shock wave . . . " is an excerpt from *Dark Sun: The Making of the Hydrogen Bomb* by Richard Rhodes. (New York: Simon & Schuster, 1995), 472.

"... the Christy core was 6.2 kilograms." Ibid, 331.

"... body burden of plutonium was set at 0.65 micrograms." This is an excerpt from "The Health Risk of Plutonium" by George Voltz. (*Los Alamos Science*, November 26, 2000) and from a quote from the Chalk River Conferences in Ontario, Canada (1949-1953).

" ....(permissible amount of plutonium) compared to a grain of salt in four cubic yards of soil ... " is an excerpt from *The Day We Lost the H-Bomb* by Barbara Moran, 145.

"... 22 milligrams if injected, 88 if inhaled ... " is an excerpt from "The Health Risk of Plutonium" by Dr. George Voelz. (*Los Alamos Science*, November 26, 2000). All information about the mortality rate and half-life data of Plutonium-239 came from this article.

Materials in Secondary came from *Broken Arrow (Vol. I).* by Maggelet & Oskins, 295-96.

Contents of Thule secondary scattered, ibid, 233.

Thule Monitor end of carrying nuclear weapons aboard alert aircraft, "No publicity is to be given this fact," and General Marshall Garth, memo, January 22, 1968, came from *15 Minutes* by Douglas Keeney, 318.

Thule Monitor to warn of power outage in ice storm. Ibid, 253.

Bunker Hill Broken Arrow secondary, "When it was moved, it ignited again." Ibid, 300.

"Plutonium rides on grains of sand ... " came from the "Human Health Fact Sheet." (Argonne National Laboratory, EVS, August 2005)

"We are not sure what is under the soil ... " is an excerpt from G. D. Gearina's article "Area 61." (*The News & Observer*, August 11, 2002)

Note on Device Testing. The first thermonuclear test on November 1, 1952, at Eniwetok Atoll was called MIKE, and an observer described it this way, in the book *Dark Sun: The Making of the Hydrogen Bomb* by Richard Rhodes:

I was stunned. I mean, it was big. I had worked out a way to calibrate the shot. I would hold up a quarter to use as a measurement to cover the fireball. As soon as I could, I whipped off my glasses and the thing was enormous, bigger than anything I'd ever imagined it would be. It looked like it blocked out the whole horizon, and I was standing on the deck of the *Estes*, thirty miles away.

MIKE was 10.4 megatons.

Notes to Chapter 6. The Cause of the Crash

" . . . C-130 carrying 452 people . . . " is an excerpt from Carl Posey's article "50 Years of Hercules." (*Air & Space/Smithsonian* Magazine, September 1, 2004)

Wet wing fuel tank information, and other wing data, including production dates of G-models came from the Global Security Web site. (www.GlobalSecurity.org/wmd/systems/b-52g)

The Comment from Mr. Michael Lombardi, Boeing Historical Research, came from an e-mail to author. (February 1, 2011)

The Officer Effectiveness Reports (OERs) of Major Tulloch were provided by Betty Tulloch, who filed her request as Next Of Kin, through National Military Records Center, St. Louis, Missouri.

Information on bombing of London as a mistake came from *15 Minutes* by Douglas Keeney, 115.

". . . If small fires to break out in paint lockers . . . " Ibid, 224.

". . . If we do this overflight right . . . " is an excerpt from the RAND Report, as quoted by Paul Lahmar in "Stranger Than Strangelove, A General's Foray In the Nuclear Zone."

". . . The whole idea is to kill the bastards . . . " is an excerpt from the RAND Report, as reported by William Kaufman of *The Boston Globe.* (2008)

The story about Eisenhower's *predelegation* is from *15 Minutes* by Douglas Keeney, 180. Except for the quote on Double Secret Probation—that is the author's.

". . . Power was mean, cruel . . . not stable . . ." was quoted from Horace Wade from *Dark Sun* by Richard Rhodes, 571.

Part II. Aftermath

Notes to Chapter 7. After Goldsboro

" . . . .ARM/SAFE switch controlled by Radar/Navigator . . ." is an excerpt from the "Plumber/Greenwood Report." (Sandia Report 98-1184C.)

The example of Mylar capacitor as weak link in fireset came from *Building the Bombs* by Charles Lowber, 154.

Notes On the Two Mistakes:

October 24, 1962, Volk Field, Wisconsin. ". . . an interesting event" came from *One Minute to Midnight* by Michael Dobbs, 132.

". . . June 3 and 6, 1980. An alarm indicating a massive Soviet missile attack . . ." is an excerpt from Shaun Gregory's *The Hidden Cost of Deterrence: Nuclear Weapons Accidents*. (Brassey's UK, London, 1990), 178.

Information on the Yuba City Broken Arrow came from Broken Arrow (Vol 1) by Maggelet & Oskins, 173.

". . . making the Faro site 'safe' . . ." is an excerpt from "1-24-61-Goldsboro, North Carolina Accident #21," from the Los Alamos National Laboratory Archives and History Programs, obtained by Paul Dotson. (Declassified report, June 18, 2004)

Information on the Chernobyl half-dome came from the article "New Tomb for an Old Disaster." (*Popular Mechanics*, May 2011)

". . . Fukushima Daiichi would mean millions of new cancers . . ." is an excerpt from the article "Unsafe At Any Dose," by Helen Caldicott, MD. (*The New York Times*, May 1, 2011)

". . . Browns Ferry . . . worst nuclear accident until Three Mile Island. . ." is an excerpt from the article, "The Fire at the Browns Ferry Nuclear Power Station," by David Dinsmore Comey, excerpted from *Not Man Apart*. (Friends of the Earth, 1976)

Information about Thermo-Lag and the Davis-Besse nuclear plant came from the article "Nuclear Agency Beset By Lapses," by Tom Zeller, Jr. (*The New York Times*, May 8, 2011)

Notes on Declassified information about nuclear weapons is published from time to time by the Department of Energy Office of Declassification. Their report "RDD-7," from January 1, 2001, on page 55 is the following:

(Certain declassified facts include): t. Special nuclear materials masses: That about 6 kg plutonium is enough hypothetically to make one nuclear explosive device. (93-2)

Followed by: NOTE: The average masses of special nuclear materials in the US nuclear weapons or special nuclear materials masses in any specific weapon type remain classified.

In other words, hypothetically we can't tell you how much plutonium is in specific weapons, but here is the minimum it would take to detonate.

Notes on Size of Secondary came from Dr. Jack ReVelle who said he never knew what was in the *black box* of a secondary, he did not have the need to know, just how to render it safe. But he described this secondary as about 14" wide, 35" long, and weighing between 200 and 300 pounds.

New Invention. An official requirement for a new invention came out of the 1961 incident. Attempts to locate the secondary were not successful by using the two devices then in service, the AN/PRS-3 and the Forster Bomb Locator, which was borrowed from the US Naval EOD Technical Center. The requested new device would have to have the capabilities of locating— down to fifty feet in soil—three types of material: ferrous material, non-ferrous material contained in a nuclear weapon, and radioactive material. It must also be man-portable, rugged, *tropicalized* and water-resistant, and easily assembled by the operator, among other requirements. And show the depth to fifty feet. (Airmunitions Letter No. 136-11-56Gm, April 18, 1962.)

Seymour Johnson Air Force Base is the only Air Force Base in the world named after a Navy aviator. The man Seymour Johnson was a Goldsboro native who died in a plane crash in 1940, and Seymour Johnson Field was named after him. It was closed after the war and reopened in 1956 as a Tactical Air Command Air Force base, Two years later the Strategic Air

Command came to Seymour Johnson in the form of the 4241st Strategic Wing, the unit of *Keep 19*. In 1963, it was redesignated the Sixty-eighth Bomb Wing, and utilized B-52 bombers and KC-135 tankers. The SAC Wing was on base for twenty-four years from 1958 to 1982, when SAC was deactivated. Today, the base is home of the Fourth Fighter Wing.

Captain Taylor Valentine and his EOD team at Seymour Johnson Air Force Base invited Jack ReVelle and me to visit them in their place of business. They were kind enough to give us a tour of the EOD shop on base. To hear these young warriors talk to a guy who deactivated two thermonuclear bombs a few miles away and fifty years ago was an amazing event. Those guys have some really ugly-looking toys in their inner sanctum, collected the hard way. Captain Valentine is today's counterpart of Jack ReVelle, fifty years later. A photo of this historic event is below. Thanks to all those young men and women for their service to our country.

2011 EOD Team, Seymour Johnson Air Force Base, Goldsboro, North Carolina, with Dr. Jack ReVelle.

It should be noted that all material used has gone through the official and lengthy declassification process. No classified material is used. Here I will quote **some very good advice** by Lieutenant Colonel Derek Duke, USAF, (Retired), that he stated in his book *Chasing Loose Nukes:* "This is a work of non-fiction. However, since loose nukes fall into the category of Weapons of Mass Destruction, I occasionally found it necessary to alter/and or omit certain aspects of their design . . . Nitpicking critics are advised to get over it and move on."

Bibliography of References

B-52 Stratofortress History. "B-52 Stratofortress," accessed June 21, 2011, http://www.GlobalSecurity.org/wmd/systems/b-52.htm

Boyne, Walter J. *Boeing B-52: A Documentary History*, Washington, DC, Smithsonian Institution Press, 1981.

Boyne, Walter J. "The Dawn of Discipline." *Air & Space/Smithsonian*, July 2009.

Caldicott, Helen. "Unsafe at Any Dose." *The New York Times*, May 1, 2011.

Comey, David D. *Not Man Apart: The Fire at the Browns Ferry Nuclear Power Station*. Friends of the Earth, 1976.

D'Alto, Nick. "Oldies & Oddities: Zeppo's Gizmo." *Air & Space/Smithsonian*, September 2008.

Dobbs, Michael. *One Minute to Midnight: Kennedy, Khrushchev, and Castro on the Brink of Nuclear War*. New York: Alfred A. Knopf, 2008.

Duke, Col. Derek L. *Chasing Loose Nukes, as told to Fred Dungan*. Riverside, California: Dungan Books, 2007.

Fine, K. & Herring, S. "The Bomb—One Click from Armageddon." Greensboro *News & Record*, January 23, 2011.

Gearino, G.D. "Area 61." *The News & Observer*, August 11, 2002.

"Part of Nuclear Device Embedded at Crash Scene." *The Goldsboro News-Argus*, March 21, 1961.

Government Document: *AF Form 14*, (nkd). *Report of Aircraft Accident, January 24, 1961*. Obtained through Freedom of Information Act, by Joel Dobson, August 28, 2010, from FOIA Manager, Kirtland AFB, NM.

Government Document: "Explosive Ordnance Disposal Report of a Broken Arrow Near Goldsboro, North Carolina, Wright-Patterson Air Force Base, Ohio." Lt. Jack B. ReVelle, USAF, February 6, 1961.

Government Document: "Official Observer's Report, Air Force Accident, Goldsboro, NC, *(Sanitized)*." Ross B. Speer, AEC/ALO, February 16, 1961.

Government Document: "Seymour Johnson Air Force Base Accident, Goldsboro, *N.C. W-7-2717.*" T. T. Scolman and D. R. Smith, February 20, 1961.

Government Document: *AF Form 14, Section K*, (nkd). "History of Flight, January 24, 1961." Obtained through Freedom of Information Act by Douglas Keeney.

Government Document (nkd). "Strategic Air Command Operations in the Cuban Crisis of 1962, Historical Study." (No. 90, Vol. 1), 48.

Government Document: Restricted Data Declassification "Decisions 1946 to the Present (RDD-7)." US Department of Energy Office of Declassification, January 1, 2001.

Government Document: "The Operational Side of Air Offense, B-60725." Remarks by General Curtis E. LeMay to USAF Advisory Board, May 21, 1957.

Government Document: "OOAMA Airmunitions Letter No. 136-11 56G, HQ." Ogden AMA, USAF, Hill AFB, UT, April 18, 1961.

Gregory, Shaun. "The Hidden Cost of Deterrence: Nuclear Weapons Accidents." Brassey's UK, London, 1990.

Hanauer, Gary. "The Story Behind the Pentagon's Broken Arrow." *Mother Jones* Magazine, April 1981.

Hardy, Scott. (2005). "The Broken Arrow of Camelot: An Analysis of the 1961 B-52 Crash and Loss of the Nuclear Weapon in Faro, North Carolina." (Masters Thesis, East Carolina University, 2005)

Hansen, C. "Swords of Armageddon." Last accessed June 21, 2011, http://www.ibiblio.org/bomb. CD-ROM.

Human Health Fact Sheet. "Plutonium." Argonne National Laboratory, EVS, August 2005.

The Kassel Mission of September 27, 1944. Last accessed June 21, 2011, http://www.KasselMission.com/society.htm

Keeney, D. (Producer), Youman, C. (Director). *No Easy Days: Snakes in the Cockpit*. (First Look Home Entertainment, 1998) VHS. Available from Avion Park, Jacksonville, FL.

Keeney, Douglas L. *15 Minutes: General Curtis LeMay and the Countdown to Nuclear Annihilation*. New York: St. Martin's Press, 2011.

Lapp, Ralph. *Kill and Overkill: The Strategy of Annihilation*. Basic Books, 1962.

Loeber, Charles R. *Building Bombs: A History of the Nuclear Weapons Complex*. Albuquerque, NM, Sandia National Laboratories, 2002.

Machado, Rod. *Rod Machado's Instrument Pilot's Survival Manual*. Long Beach: Aviation's Speakers Bureau, 1991.

Maggelet, Michael H. & Oskins, James C. *Broken Arrow: The Declassified History of U.S. Nuclear Weapons Accidents*. lulu.com, 2007.

Maggelet, Michael H. & Oskins, James C. *Broken Arrow, Vol II: A Disclosure of Significant* U.S., Soviet, and British Nuclear Weapon Incidents and Accidents, 1945-2008. lulu.com, 2010.

Meisler, H. *The Occurrence and Geochemistry of Salty Groundwater in the Northern Atlantic Coastal Plain*. US Geological Survey Professional Papers 1404-D, 51. Washington, DC, USCG, 1989.

Moran, Barbara. *The Day We Lost the H-Bomb: Cold War, Hot Nukes, and the Worst Nuclear Weapons Disaster in History*. New York: Random House, 2009.

Nelson, Cliff, Harrison, Nick, Leung, Andrew, & Butler, Megan. "Broken Arrow: Goldsboro, NC: The truth Behind North Carolina's Brush with Nuclear Disaster." Last accessed June 21, 2011, http://www.ibiblio.org/bomb

Nuclear Bomb Chart (n.d.), Strategic Air Command (SAC), last accessed June 21, 2011, http://www.Strategic-Air-Command.com/weapons/nuclear_bomb_chart.htm

The Nuclear Weapon Archive, A Guide To Nuclear Weapons. (n.d.), last accessed June 21, 2011, http://NuclearWeaponArchive.org

"New Tomb for Old Disaster." *Popular Mechanics* Magazine, May 2011.

Posey, Carl. "50 Years of Hercules." *Air & Space/Smithsonian* Magazine, September 1, 2004. http://www.AirSpaceMag.com/history-of-flight/hercules.html

Price, E. "Board of Inquiry to Look Into Crash." *The Goldsboro News-Argus*, July 25, 1961.

Plummer, David W. and Greenwood, William H. *The History of Nuclear Weapon Safety Devices*. Albuquerque, NM: Sandia National Laboratories, Surety Components and Instrumentation Center, 1998.

Reed, Thomas. *At the Abyss: An Insider's History of the Cold War*. New York: Presidio Press, 2004.

Rhodes, Richard. *Dark Sun: The Making of the Hydrogen Bomb*. New York: Simon & Schuster, 1995.

Sandia Corporation. "Analysis of the Safety Aspects of the [deleted] Bombs Involved in B-52 Crash Near Goldsboro, North Carolina, SCDR 81-61," as attached to letter dated March 27, 1961, to James T. Ramey, Executive Director, JCAE, from A. R. Luedecke, General Manager, USAEC, February 1961.

Sedgwick, J. "January 1961, Bombs Over Goldsboro." This Month in North Carolina History Archives, UNC Libraries, North Carolina Collection, January 2008.

Stockholm International Peace Research Yearbook, World Armaments and Disarmament. MIT Press, 1977.

Strickland, Wilton. *In the BUFF*. Self-published, 2003. http://www.WiltonStrickland.com

Voltz, G. "The Health Risk of Plutonium." *Los Alamos Science*, November 26, 2000.

Yancy, N. "Life-Death Story of Flight Told." Greensboro *News & Record*, January 26, 1961.

Zeller, Tom. "Nuclear Agency Beset by Lapses." *The New York Times*, May 8, 2011.

About the author

Joel Dobson is a former Air Force officer who was in the Strategic Air Command in the 1960s. He is now retired, and lives with his wife Judy, a former nurse, in Greensboro, North Carolina. He has a private pilot's license, with instrument rating, but does not fly anymore.

This is his first book.

Web site: TheGoldsboroBrokenArrow.com

Printed in Great Britain
by Amazon.co.uk, Ltd.,
Marston Gate.